I0836901

The Polk Street Review

2022 edition

The Gift Of An Hour

a global anthology
celebrating of Noblesville, IN

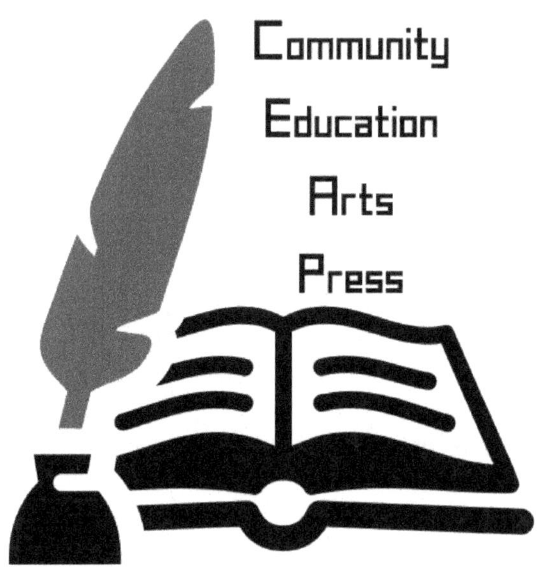

First Printing: February 2022

Cover design: Alys Caviness-Gober
Cover art: *Vacation* by Alys Caviness-Gober
Additional *art nouveau* images provided by Alys Caviness-Gober
Project design, formatting, and layout: Alys Caviness-Gober
Editors: Alys Caviness-Gober & Sarah E. Morin

ISBN: 978-0-9998858-7-1

Community • Education • Arts Press
a division of *Community • Education • Arts, Inc.*
Noblesville, IN 46060
1st Printing: February 2022
https://CEArts.org

Ordering Information:
Special discounts are available on quantity purchases by corporations, associations, educators, and others. Please contact us at info@cearts.org for details.
U.S. trade bookstores and wholesalers: please contact Alys at info@cearts.org for details.

dedicated to our families and friends

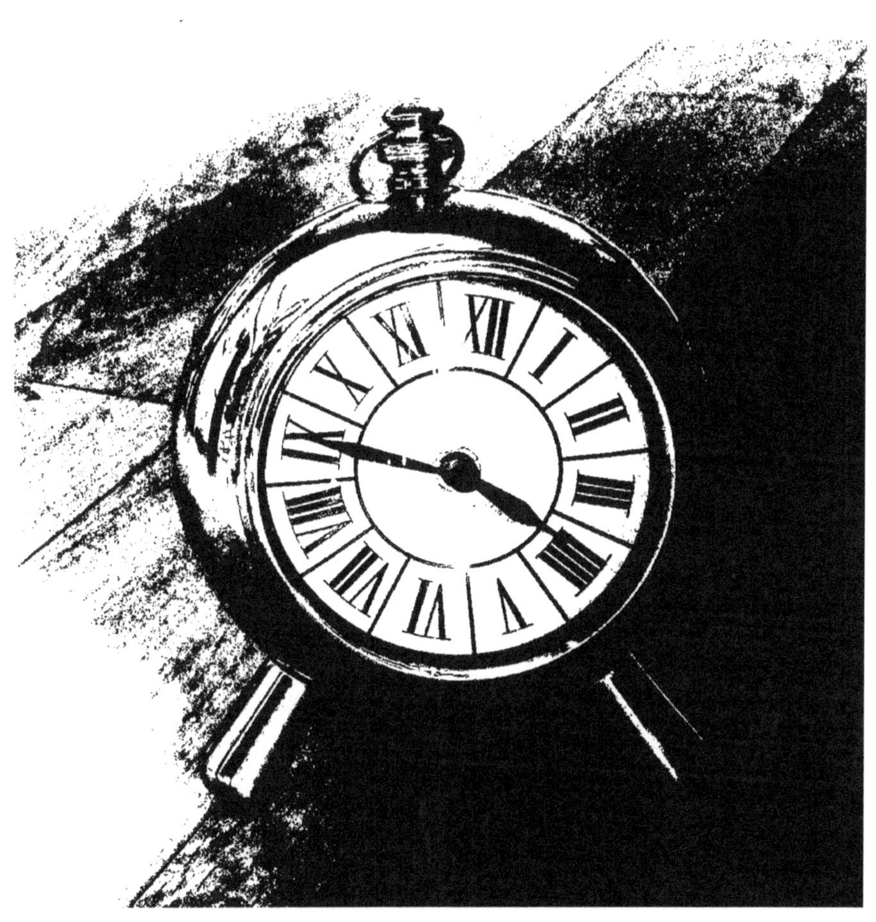

2022 Advertisers and Sponsors

We must thank our individual donors and corporate sponsors for their financial support in 2021 & 2022. Without them, neither this book nor our organization would exist.

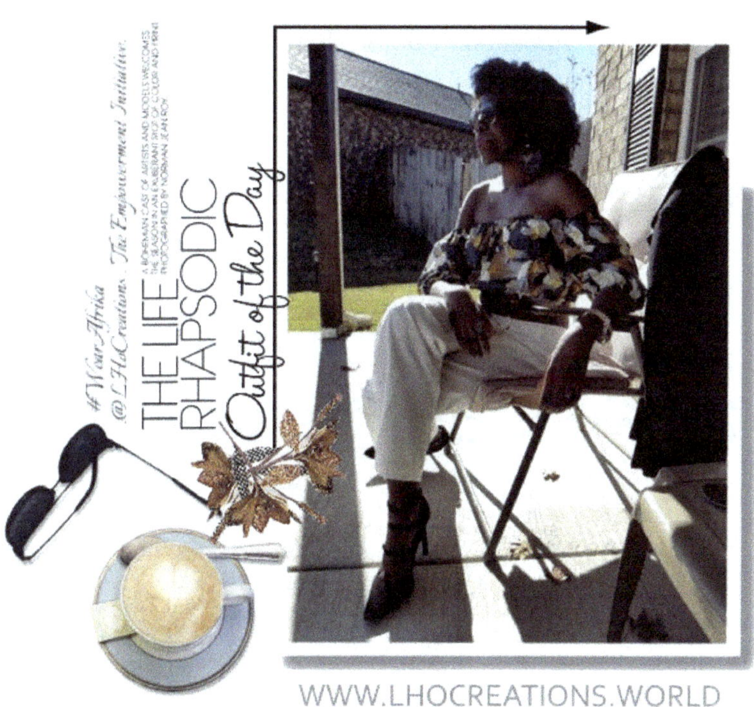

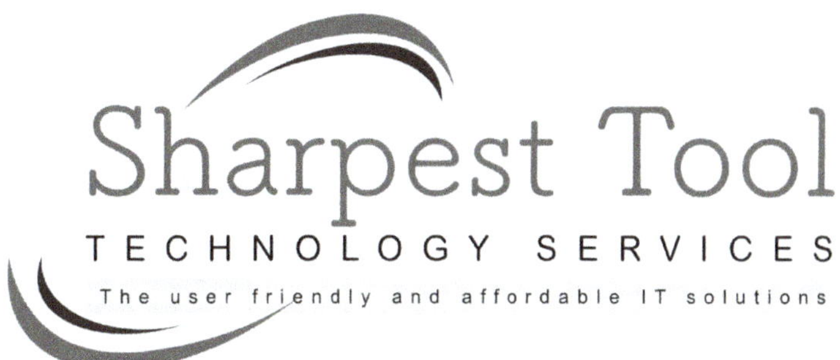

844-894-TECH (8324)
sharpesttooltech.com/

We specialize in small businesses and homes

- Networking Services
- Office 365
- Equipment Repairs
- Maintenance Plans
- Website Services

Individual Sponsors

2021-22 TPSR Directed Donations:
Jean Roberts
Chuck Kellum

Facebook Fundraisers Donors:
Alys Caviness-Gober
Emily Wasonga
Lisa Naddy
Bonita Cox Searle
Sherri Bonham

Monthly CEArts Donor:
Alys Caviness-Gober

Thank you to all who support CEArts!

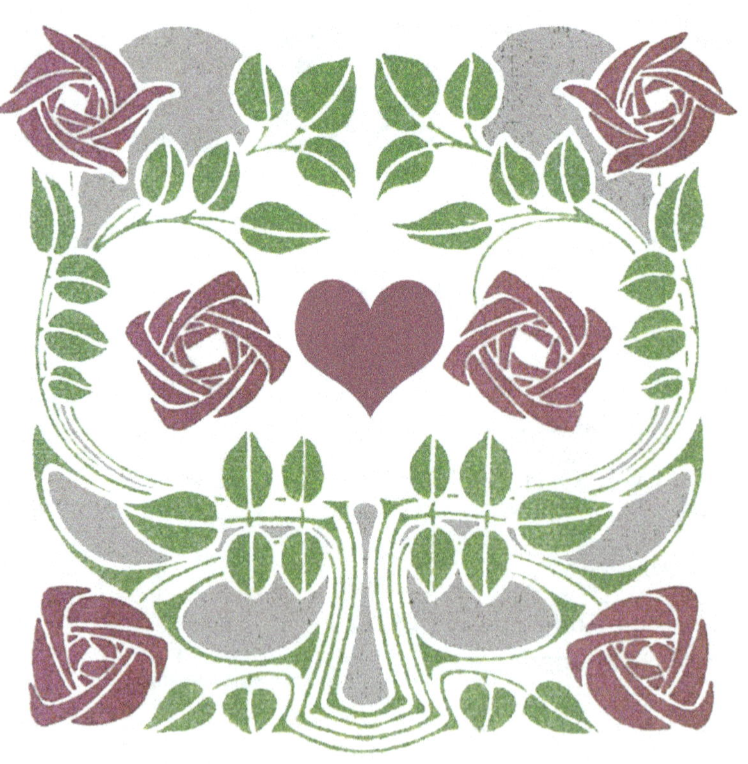

Table of Contents

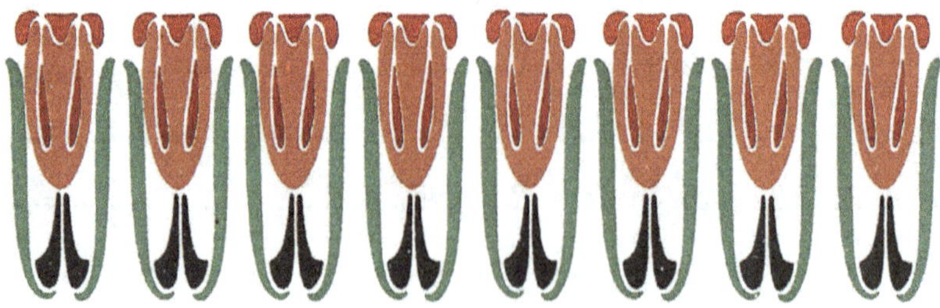

Introduction

In 2013, four years before CEArts took over publishing this annual anthology, I submitted my first piece to *The Polk Street Review*. It was the first poem I had written in years, so its inclusion meant a lot to me: the rebirth of an interest, the warming thought someone (besides my parents) cared about my writing again, and a publication credit. What I didn't expect would grow out of the experience, and has continued to grow since Alys and I took over as editors, was a connection to a community of writers and visual artists.

Indeed, in the years since, that is what has meant the most to me: the human connection. Art can be a lonely pastime. As Mary Heaton Vorse said, "The art of writing is the art of applying the seat of the pants to the seat of the chair." That chair is often in a blessedly isolated corner, if you can snatch it. Are creatives solitary birds, like the blue heron, or a noisy vee of geese, honking encouragement at each other as we journey? After we steep in the aloneness necessary for concentration, many of us crave time with an artistic flock. Many of the people I met that first time I attended a launch of *The Polk Street Review* became my creative gaggle: we critiqued each other in writers' groups, partnered in collaborations, bought each other's works, left each other a thumbs up and encouraging comment on social media as we celebrated successes and vented about creative blocks.

The pandemic has proven a challenge to that keystone of *The Polk Street Review*'s sense of union: our in-person launch. This will be our second edition launched on Zoom. While I would far rather mingle with my fellow/sister creatives over cheese and crackers, I still look forward to cheering on each presenter onscreen and in the chatbox. Although through the repeated editing process I have become deeply intimate with the creative punctuation of some of our submitters, there's still nothing like hearing someone read or discuss their own work. Even in these challenging times, *The Polk Street Review* remains what it always was: a place to celebrate writers and artists.

Perhaps in my mind that is what has always set this anthology apart. We are a community as much as a publication, a community that now reaches beyond Noblesville, Indiana to other continents. We welcome contributors from as far away as Africa as honorary residents of our artistic borough. For the past several years, we have encouraged our submitters to think globally through a special international connection section. This year, we have woven those pieces throughout the body of the anthology. You will see a globe symbol 🌎 when a piece steps outside our own country or was sent by a creator outside the United States.

As editors, Alys and I try to clarify meaning or fix an odd capitalization here or there, but our goal has always been not to tamper too much with the voice of the writer. Except when we felt necessary, we have chosen to respect our contributor's artistic choices. Sometimes that means publishing pieces with viewpoints very different from our own. Sometimes we have updated language to reflect what we see as best modern inclusive practice, and sometimes we have chosen to let verbiage stand, such as in historical pieces. We hope we have struck the difficult balance between respecting the intent of the author and respecting any marginalized groups mentioned in the published pieces. Inclusion is one of our core values at CEArts, and we have learned our own journey in that process is ever evolving. We beg forgiveness for any editorial interference that left too much said or too much unsaid.

We have again selected award winners in each of the following categories: *Poetry and Lyrics*, *Prose*, and *Artwork Images*. The selection process is both a joy and a punishment. How are Alys and I supposed to choose between so many excellent pieces, when all deserve recognition? But after much discussion, we found pieces in each category that stood out to us, in our own subjective option. We applaud these artists and writers for their high degree of craftsmanship and creative use of theme, and invite you to view the list of winners at the back of the book. Please note two additional awards: *Special Award* and *Award of Merit*. A *Special Award* goes to one or more contributors who have given *The Polk Review* something that cannot be captured by the other prizes, but deserves recognition.The *Award of Merit* is our Best in Book out of all submitted pieces.

We hope you as reader enjoy your time spent here in our community of artists and writers.

About TPSR Theme

A few years ago, we made the theme an optional prompt for submissions, and added a theme contest to our annual TPSR project. This time around we received many great theme ideas; selecting from the submissions was tough. The 2022 edition of *The Polk Street Review* winning theme, submitted by someone who wishes to remain anonymous, comes from this quote:

Reverie is not a mind vacuum. It is rather the gift of an hour which knows the plenitude of the soul.

~ Gaston Bachelard,
La poétique de la rêverie
(*The Poetics of Reverie*) (1969), Ch. 2, sect. 3

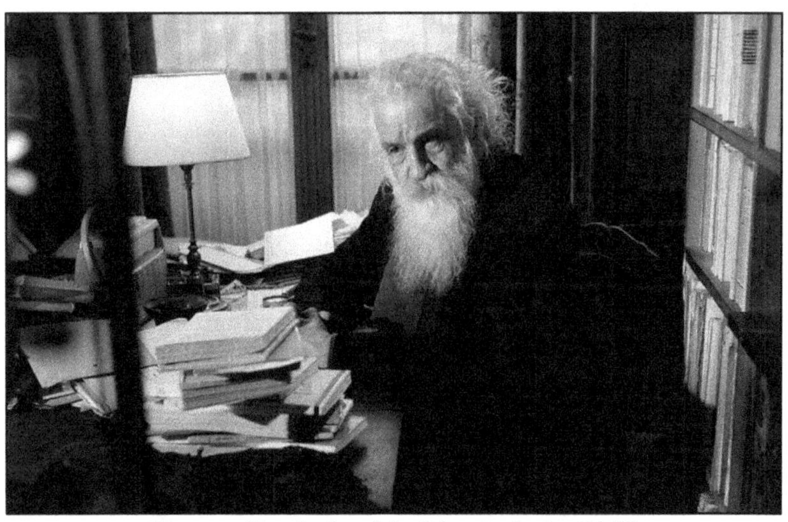

Gaston Bachelard in his study in 1961.
Photo by Bernard Pascucci/INA/Getty

After we chose the theme, we did a little research on Gaston Bachelard. He was an intriguing man, a bit ahead of his time in some areas, and altogether interesting enough that we wanted to include some information about him in this edition.

Gaston Bachelard (27 June 1884 – 16 October 1962) was a French philosopher, contributing to the fields of poetics and the philosophy of science. His areas of interest included historical epistemology, constructivist epistemology, history and philosophy of science, philosophy of art, phenomenology, psychoanalysis, literary theory, and education.

Bachelard was also a Feminist philosopher. Going against sexist stereotypes of the time, he ensured his daughter Suzanne was well-educated; she became a mathematician and philosopher who developed well-respected phenomenological and epistemological research.

Bachelard's works include *Le nouvel esprit scientifique* (1934; *The New Scientific Spirit*), *La formation de l'esprit scientifique* (*The Formation of the Scientific Mind,* 1938), *La psychanalyse du feu* (1938; *The Psychoanalysis of Fire*, English language publication 1964), *L'eau et les rêves* (1942; *Water and Dreams*, English language publication 1983), and *The Poetics of Space* (1958). *La poétique de la rêverie* (1958; *The Poetics of Reverie: Childhood, Language, and the Cosmos*, 1969) was published for the first time in an English translation seven years after Bachelard's death in 1962.

Author Gillian Darley says of Bachelard:

In his Poetics of Space, Gaston Bachelard created a philosophy of at-homeness, rich in emotion and memory . . . he guides us through an actual or imagined home (your choice), its comforts and mysteries, assembled and brought into focus, in a place and at a time undefined except by the limits of our own daydreams, longings and memories – those inner landscapes from which, he said, new worlds can be made. The philosopher evokes an idealised past, places the miniature against the immense, and guides us back into childhood. Once there, at home, he reminds us how we tend to look down the cellar stairs, apprehensively, while gazing upwards, towards the attic, always eager. Uncertainty is set against promise, dark against light. This house is a key to an inner self, 'for childhood is certainly greater than reality'.

from *Intimate spaces*
by Gillian Darley, 17 October 2017
https://aeon.co/essays/how-gaston-bachelard-gave-the-emotions-of-home-a-philosophy

Our theme, *The Gift Of An Hour,* feels both relevant and poignant amidst the global pandemic. How many of us were granted or denied the gift of an hour with a loved one before they passed? What wouldn't we give for one more hour with them? We won't ever again take for granted the gift of an hour with a parent, grandparent, brother, sister, son, daughter, or beloved grandchild. How many of us will never again take for granted the gift of an hour congregating with friends at a local art gallery or a neighborhood bar, or listening to a singer-songwriter perform live, or the relaxation of going out to eat, or the wonder of witnessing weddings, or the sorrow of saying goodbye at funerals? In each of those settings, the gift of an hour is precious. Our hours, alone or with others, have perhaps changed forever.

As we go to print with this edition of our annual anthology, we are still in a global pandemic in which Indiana ranks first as the most dangerous state to be in due to our low vaccinated percentage and high COVID-19 case numbers. Too many of our fellow Hoosiers still aren't taking seriously the virus and its many variants, but we are grateful to those who have been fully vaccinated and continue to use protective measures like mask-wearing and social distancing. Their vigilance protects all of us.

Because we don't know what the hours of 2022 will look like, we ask ourselves: *how best can CEArts fill the gift of an hour? How best can we help others savor the gift of an hour?*

At *Community • Education • Arts*, we're doing what we can to answer both questions by offering diverse arts opportunities and projects for creatives of all kinds to share their artwork. *The Polk Street Review* is one of those projects. We're grateful to our sponsors and to the people who sent us their wonderful creations.

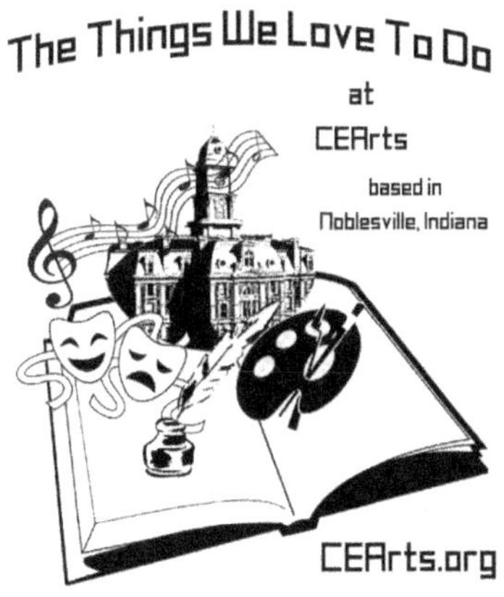

Poems 'Round the Clock: Twelve Brief Reflections on Time *a collaborative poem by Noble Poets*

David Allen, John A. Caviness, Alys Caviness-Gober, B. Monét (Natalie Gaytan), Z. Rose (Payge Gillig), Chuck Kellum, Sarah E. Morin, Mike Nierste, Paul "Spike" Wilson

I

Bygone memories, ticked
presented by one
gifted, gone but carried
steal away an hour of your day
give it away in counts of sixty.

II

How arbitrary, this unit.
An hour is 1/24 of your day or 4.16666% (6s into infinity).
Google credits ancient Egyptians and their star-gazing eyes,
so obsessed with celestial dance and death
they wrote time tables inside coffin lids.
Why do the dead need to tell time?
Whisper from beyond how time and infinity blend.

III

No use
rummaging in your purse for the receipt.
An hour cannot be taken back.
Will you squander or hoard
this clock-shaped coin,
this non-refundable purchase?

IV

Tick-tock.
Minutes multiply mindlessly.
The room drips away.

V

We waited, as time stopped:
this gift, this time, with you,
precious as a shooting star.

VI

Metered minutia of magical moments
built in counts of sixty
only extra when it nearly hits me
passed between two
cherished in the moments.
Hour upon hour is given –
Day upon day is received –
Year upon year is shared.

VII

If only we could leap
to the beginning of the tragedy
and change the fatal end.
Instead we comment
on what happened.
Insufficient crying-face emojis
are our cartoonish Greek chorus.

VIII

Would I wish for erasure or regret –
justifications of lackluster reason?
Unable to pass on,
the sod seals the memories.

IX

Who forced an hour to be so fleeting or foreboding?
What are you left with at its end?
An hour becomes eternity when it becomes a memory.

X

Finger-painted anticipation
of hosting a toddler's birthday party –
the celebration colorful, smeared everywhere.
Glorious destruction of my living room,
my eardrums,
my patience.
Cherished milestones are also
a monkey's paw.

XI
An hour orphans words:
leftovers
of what I meant to say.

XII
What is the exchange rate –
a blind coffee date,
a day spent young, with noiseless promise,
compared to
a sleepy golden afternoon holding hands with
a partner of fifty years?
These moments are not currency to be traded
but opposite spokes
in the turning of the wheel.

Midwinter *by Mairéad Lewis* 

When Earth tilted away from the sun
– the farthest all year –
through *Meán Geimhridh*
she stood braced
against the hard unsteadiness of
bruises and
cold remnants of
the broken china –
her mother's mother's china.

When Earth tilts away from the sun
– the farthest all year –
through *Meán Geimhridh*
she stands braced
keeping vigil through
this tilting night
remembering that
darkness,
waiting for the newborn Sun.

(*Meán Geimhridh*: Celtic Midwinter, pronounced *mean guym-rid*)

***A White Bird on a Flowered Branch** by Jerry Dreesen*

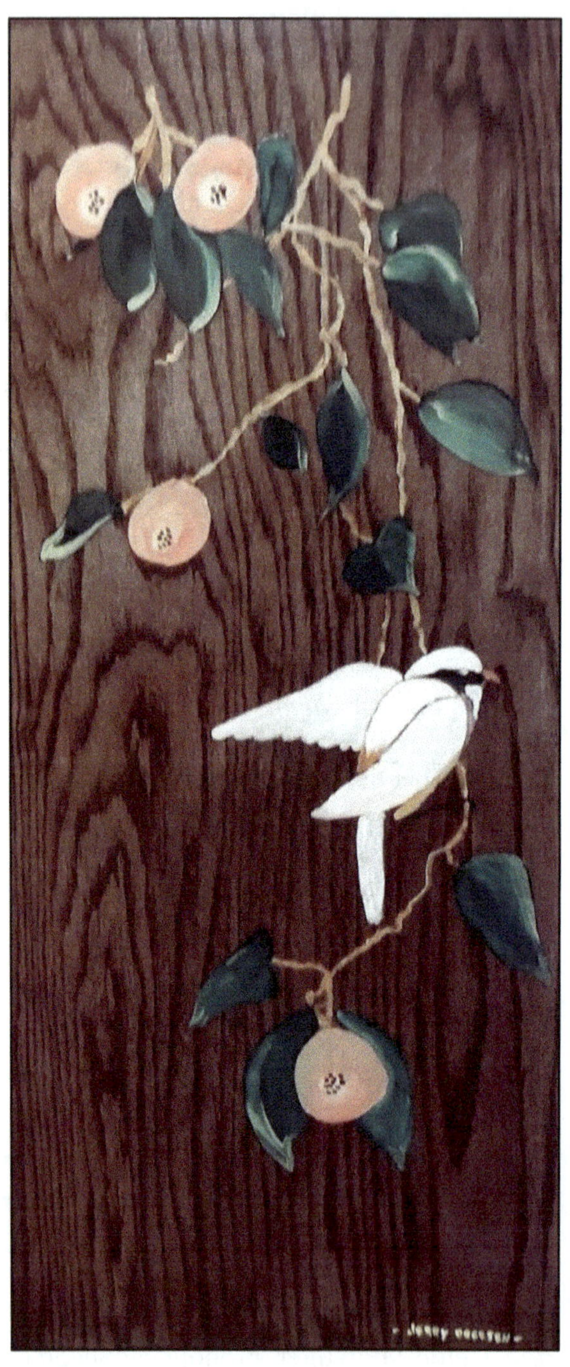

The Gift of an Hour with Grandkids, A Collection of Senryū and Haiku *by Mike Nierste*

A collection of *haiku* and *senryu* with the theme of *the gift of an hour* – these *senryū* and *haiku* reflect various treasured hours – gifts spent with grandkids.

go light, stop light,
go light, stop light, go light, stop
boo boo bear

on the waterslide
a little girl
wets her pants

summer breeze
the wind chime
of playground swings

digesting
a magazine
literally

snack time
the cheerio kid
shoots 'em down

potty time again
this time we get
two chocolate chips

pedaling a trike
around the great expanse
of the cul-de-sac

reading out loud
story time makes
the pictures perfect

nap time in soft beds
under cover spies
just teddy bears

elderberry juice
smoothies – not so smooth
on carpeting

A Gift of Parental Love *by Kristine Staley* 

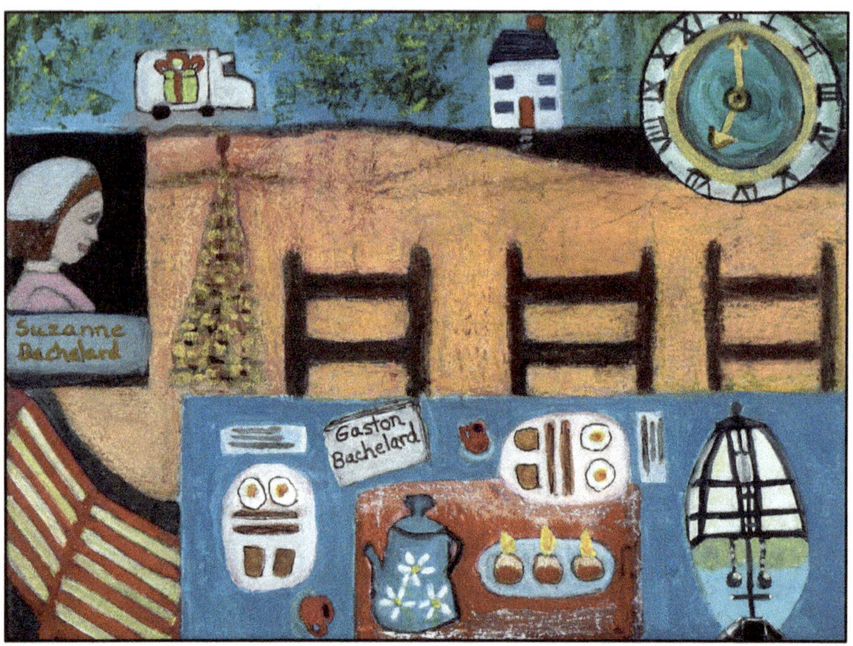

The theme of this painting is the love Gaston Bachelard showed his daughter Suzanne. She is the one pictured in the painting on the left. She is overlooking a breakfast table she shared with her father. The dining table represents a location for family values to be shared, careers planned, and the definition of a successful life. The table is set for breakfast at 7AM and reflects the importance of a family meal and sharing that hour of time.

The Gift is given to both Suzanne and her father. Suzanne was given the gift of self-confidence to pursue a teaching career in Mathematics which was an unusual choice for a female for her time. Bachelard was recognized for his beliefs in feminism and gender equality. Equality is represented by the two strips of bacon on each plate. The angel pictured in the painting is intended to show Suzanne succeeding in self-actualization. The home pictured in the middle top symbolizes the importance of family life and the clock places them in time and space.

Professor Bachelard was given the gift of helping his child realize her dreams and he also earned degrees in physics, chemistry, and philosophy. The book on the table with Bachelard's name represents his accomplishment as an author. Underneath the table is a title of one of his books, *La Poetique de la reverie*. Gaston Bachelard's gift to his daughter and to his readers is shown by how time spent with loved ones results in the fulfillment of dreams.

Poetry *by Mona Mehas*

Poetry is reverie, say the bards.
Always lost in thought; daydreaming; in trance.
Woolgathering through life, inattention
to reality, the intricate dance.

Wandering through my life of fantasy,
poetry is reverie, say the bards.
Impractical, they say; your life in shards.
Preoccupation with my dream; escape.

Visions of writing, musings, I create.
Impressions, emotions touch my poems.
Poetry is reverie, say the bards.
Idealistic, they condemn; light weight.

Hallucination, kindly to my soul.
Abstraction, ward off the dark naysayers.
Embrace ideas; forsake outside control.
Poetry is reverie, say the bards.

Winter On The Mountains *by Jerry Dreesen*

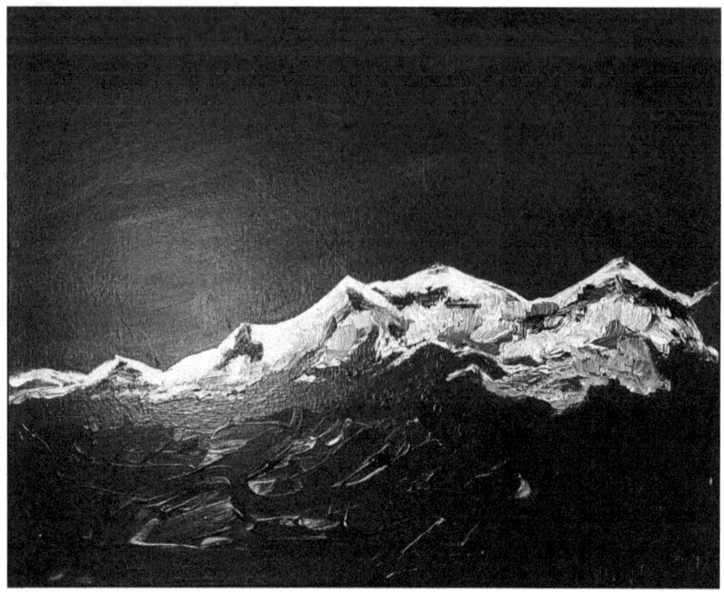

This Hour *by Deborah Petersen*

Let me take this hour
to bake you a cake:
chocolatey
light
sweet.

Let me bake you a cake
because I love you
because it makes you happy
because it is my small way
to thank you
to grow with you
to leave the shadow and scent of a memory
filled with fondness
to strengthen our bonds
as we weave together our lives,
our forever time –
let me take this hour.

untitled 1 *by B. Monét*

off the rocker – nuts
tocking the ticks of the clock
time slipping and lost

An Hour Drive with My Brother *by Leah Leach*

I spent most of my childhood jealous of my brother. From the moment he arrived home from the hospital I guessed my life would suck from then on. There is an infamous photo of me holding my infant brother, patting his head, gritting my teeth, and calculating where I could find the nearest band of gypsies to take him away.

Yeah, sure, he was cute. Big brown eyes and a perfectly round face, blah…blah…blah…. He was the first male grandchild; he was the one who would pass on the family name. He got all of Mom's and Dad's attention and well, you could say I had my moments of sabotage.

Now, I don't remember this story, but I was *told* that when I especially wanted attention, I would sit in the family room and hurl myself back and forth in the rocking chair. All my anger, all my spite got that rocking chair a-movin' until it would slam into the picture window.

> *Wack! Wack! Wack!*
> Until Mom came.
> Then I was told to stop.
> And I got in trouble.

Anyway, my brother Dan and I would continue this rivalry until it escalated into actual physical fights. One fist fight was because he threw up on my Care Bear. Silly how these things start, but I know that there was one thing we never seemed to fight about – movies.

The summer we got a VCR was the best! We had three video tapes; Dan and I on the *Bozo Show*, and *Back to the Future* and *Return of the Jedi.* I swear the invention of the VCR brought Dan and me closer together. To this day, we can repeat every word of *Back to the Future* and *Return of the Jedi.* Movies became a second language to us. We'd be able to ramble off a line from a movie and totally know what each other was talking about. Other kids had pig-Latin, we had movie lines.

Dan seemed to like the comedies best. I liked the dramas. Eventually, that started to divide us and soon we saw fewer and fewer movies together. Plus, once I got my license, I was out seeing movies with friends, and the brother-sister movie nights were becoming a thing of the past.

My friends didn't share the same passion for movies and all things pop culture as my brother and I did. My friends were more interested in boys, gossip, and fashion. I started to miss the days of watching movies over and over until I had each one perfectly memorized, so that I'd have perfect quips for future conversational moments.

Maybe that's why before I left for California I wanted to go see a movie with my brother. I let him pick. He opted for the Mike Myer's flick, *So I Married an Axe Murder,* playing at the second-run movie theater (aka the dollar theater).

Now this is back when I didn't laugh aloud in movie theaters. I didn't want to show emotion in public, and I was worried I'd ruin someone else's time. Same theory for crying in public. It took 40 years to get over this, but *So I Married an Axe Murder* was one of the few movies that I remember feeling free to laugh out loud. Maybe it was because there were other people laughing, maybe it was because there weren't many people in the theater, or perhaps it was because I was with my brother.

The movie's plot was simple. Charlie (played by Mike Myers) is a coffeehouse poet. After many failed relationships, he finds the woman of his dreams. But everything is not as it appears. Harriett (played by Nancy Travis) is a butcher who may be Mrs. X, a woman who kills her husbands on their wedding nights.

The movie had a good build to it, not funny all at once, just gems of classic one-liners and a cast of memorable characters, like Mike Myer's crazy Scottish father (also played by Mike Myers). I don't know how many times I've referenced this movie when I go to Kentucky Fried Chicken. It's impossible not to. With great lines to quote like:

> **Stuart Mackenzie**: Well, it's a well known fact, Sonny Jim, that there's a secret society of the five wealthiest people in the world, known as The Pentavirate, who run everything in the world, including the newspapers, and meet tri-annually at a

secret country mansion in Colorado, known as The Meadows.
Tony Giardino: So who's in this Pentavirate?
Stuart Mackenzie: The Queen, The Vatican, The Gettys, The Rothschilds, *and* Colonel Sanders before he went tits up. Oh, I hated the Colonel with 'is wee *beady* eyes, and that smug look on his face. "Oh, you're gonna buy my chicken! Ohhhhh!"
Charlie Mackenzie: Dad, how can you hate "The Colonel"?
Stuart Mackenzie: Because he puts an addictive chemical in his chicken that makes ya crave it fortnightly, smartass!

The movie showcases San Francisco in all its glory, from the opening image of the Bay Bridge cut to the brilliant music of The Boo Radleys to its nod to the beat generation. I was big into William Burroughs at the time, so I dug the beat references and jabs at spoken word poetry. Along with cementing the fact that Mike Myers is the funniest person of our generation, the movie also had an amazing soundtrack. From *There She Goes* by The Boo Radleys to *Saturday Night* by the Bay City Rollers, it was a cassette tape (yes, I said cassette tape) that never left my car. Well, until its fateful melting accident some years later. But before its demise I got my money's worth out of that soundtrack.

I moved from Rockford, Michigan to Vacaville, California a few weeks after seeing *Axe Murder* with my brother. Vacaville is a small town in the suburbs of the Travis Air Force Base, halfway between Sacramento and San Francisco. I loved going into San Francisco, saw lots of great movies there. I would go to the old art deco theaters with the real velvet curtains and painted frescos. There was only one problem; I was always seeing movies alone. New to town and working constantly to afford my new apartment, I didn't have a whole bunch of time to socialize, so I went to see my "movie friends." There they were any night of the week, 40 feet high, there to help me to learn to laugh, cry, and remember. I did however miss my brother. I should have been missing my friends, ex-boyfriends, or parents, but I really missed my brother.

I worked at two video stores in Vacaville. In the morning at Eastman Video, I wore a ridiculous tuxedo shirt and bowtie – and if that wasn't bad enough – a cummerbund. At night I gladly changed into normal clothes and headed to the mall to work at Suncoast Video. People at both my jobs knew movies but they didn't really *know* movies. They weren't as obsessed as my brother and I were. They didn't get my random movie references. My brother did.

Dan came out to visit during Christmas break. People thought it was weird I was all excited to see my brother. They didn't know what I had planned; and really, I think if I would have told them, they wouldn't have understood anyway.

I picked Dan up from San Francisco International Airport and we started the hour-long drive towards my place in Vacaville. I waited until the Bay Bridge was in sight. Seeing something he had only seen in a movie, my brother's eyes lit up. I popped in the *Axe Murder* soundtrack; the horns touted that unmistakable overture. Then the beat – *dun. dun. dun* and *There She Goes* by The Boo Radleys filled the car and poured onto the streets of San Francisco. Without saying a thing we both replayed the opening scene of the movie. It was my way of showing my brother, here movies come to life.

Three Pumpkins *by Mairéad Lewis*

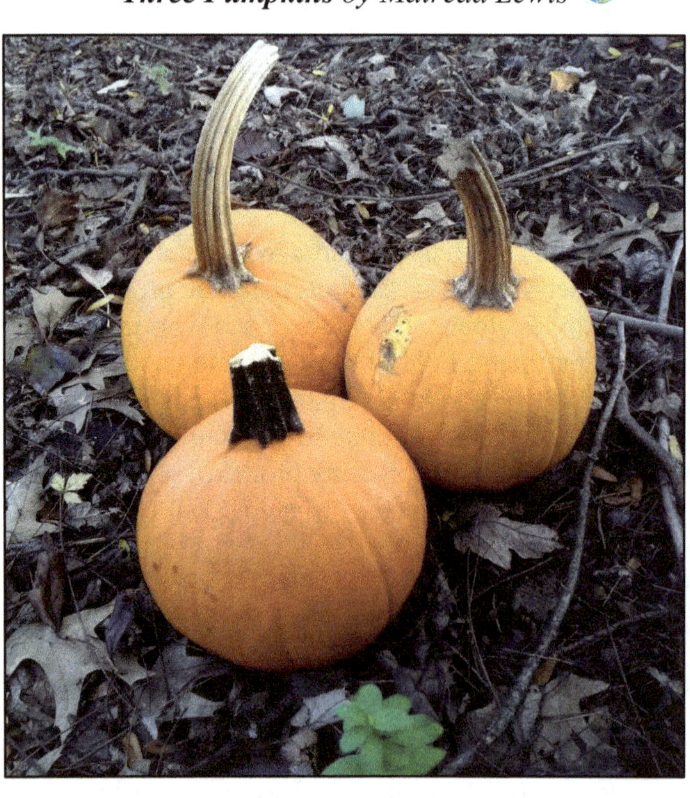

Anima Realized *by Kristine Staley*

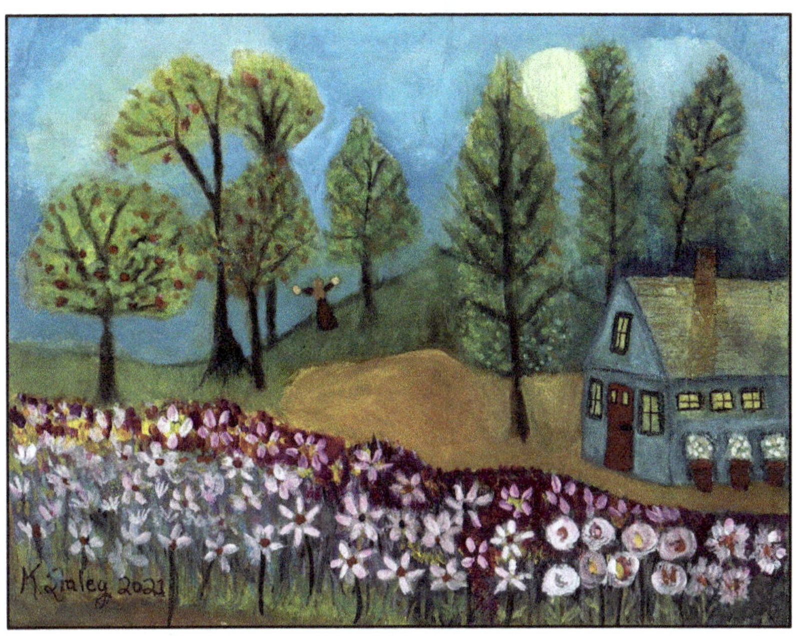

The theme of this painting reflects a dreamer returning to her beloved home and garden. Anima is a female dreamer who loves nature, art, and gardening, and is at peace feeling the tranquility of home. The trees are fruit bearing apple trees. She sustains herself, is independent, and self-sufficient. She has had her career, outside the home, and now it is time to rest and relax and simply be in the moment.

A Cute Queenly Choreographer *by Ndaba Sibanda* 

she lurks on social platforms
like a dazzling mermaid born
in the lake of high-tech and info

her movements in dance or staged dance
are descendants of real royalty and ease
a colossal appetite for soul and *mbaqanga*

she epitomizes art or practice of designing
choreographic sequences, as she marches
a march of history that glows with memories
her dance compositions are an archaeology of diaries

that sail with my mind to the Christmases of yesteryear
her moves collaborate in real time with a seamless skill

The Earthquake's Miraculous Survivor *by Ndaba Sibanda*

Retrieved from a rumbling, riotous rubble,
a cheerful child crooned that God is able.

Across the Street from Salvation *by Jenny Kalahar*

Across the street lies salvation.
A discouraged mother sits on this side, on a bus bench,
her hands stuffed into a brown cloth bag of crochet yarn,
needle held loosely.
Frown lines deepen as a cloud of emotion covers her eyes.
I have not been enough, not done enough,
not given enough to make up for being
the only daughter in a family of men.
I ache to rest, rest, rest,
but my god is awake and waiting
for me to complete unknown tasks.

My father stands somewhere in the middle of the street
reading a book of life he'd read before but has mostly forgotten.
Friends I used to know wave to me from the shadow of angels' robes,
in that way that neither encourages visitation nor waves me away,
and I am tired
but cannot sleep while my god is awake,
and I cannot remain alert in the confusing space inside my head.

Hungry for more at last,
my mother pulls her vein-lined hands from her spirals of yarn
and briefly grips my shoulders before crossing over.
My father, ever her mate, crosses shortly thereafter.
His book sits in the street,
its pages ruffling from the breeze of angels' wings,
whispering barely audible words that do not judge me,

only recite selected passages.
My friends turn toward the hazy yellow sky until they vanish,
leaving only a blended perfume of ink and home baking and sunshine.
Unprotected, I watch as my god shrinks to a mere mustard seed
resting on olive leaves
where he had once appeared so large.
Realization comes: I can choose to pick it up
and carry it faithfully as I continue on my way,
or I can ignore it,
always wondering if I've forever left salvation
on the other side of the street.

untitled 1 *by Z. Rose*

hands down, on the hour
free me from his hourglass
memory of time

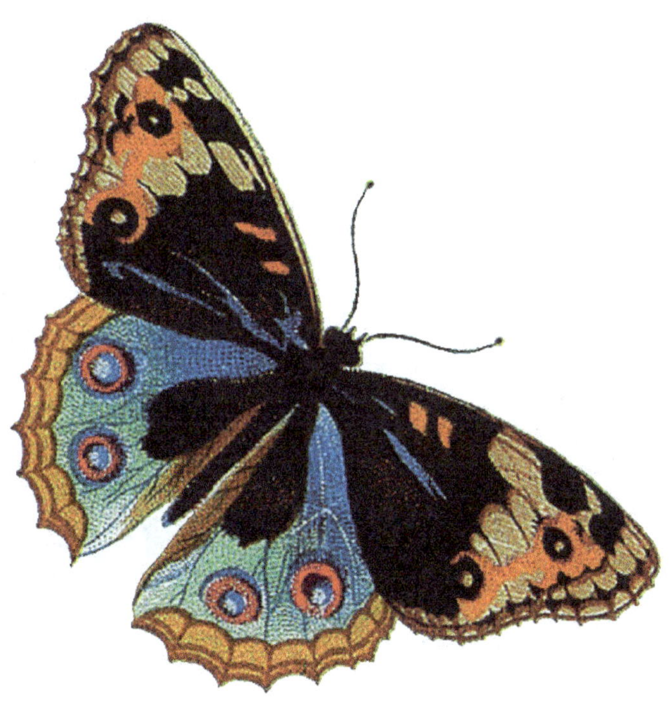

Beautiful Woman In A Hajib *by Jerry Dreesen* 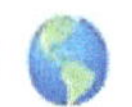

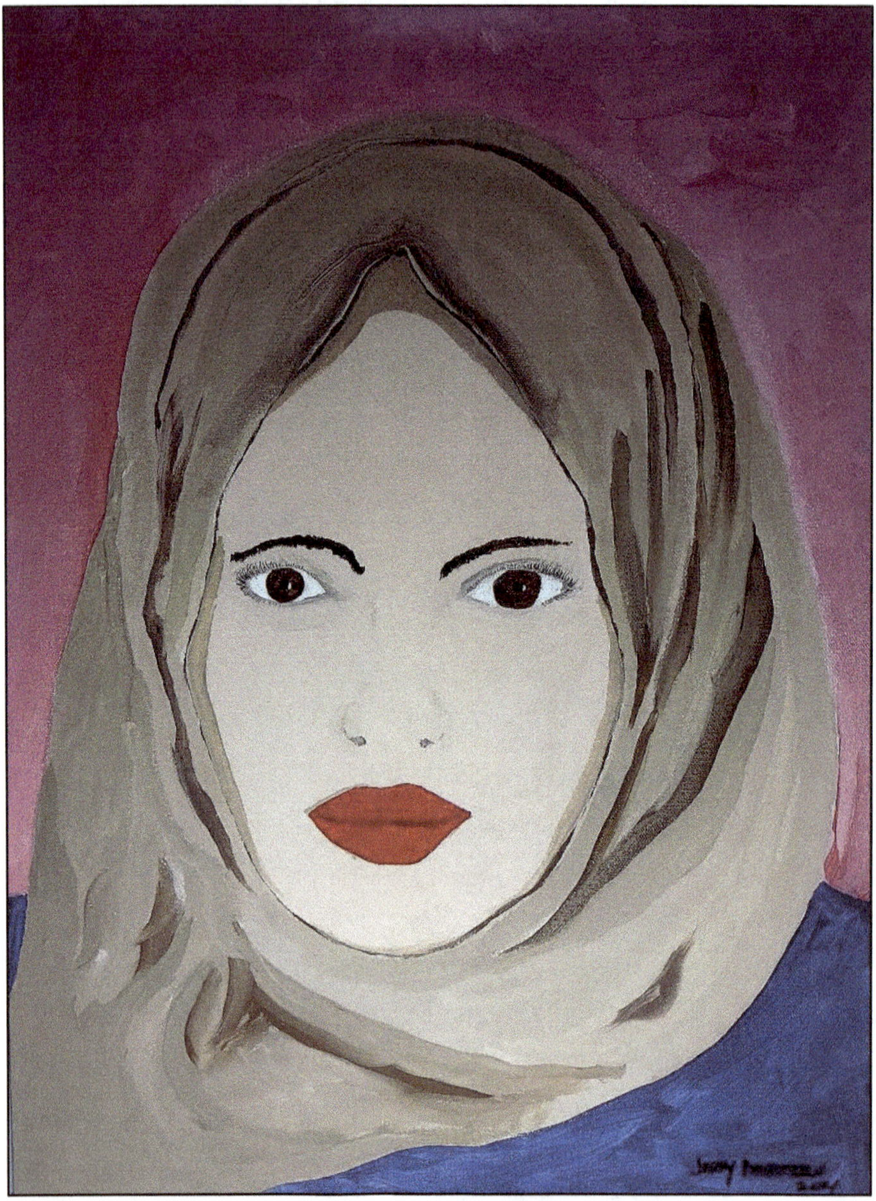

Rails and Rough Hands Remembered *by Marilyn J Wolf*

We lie in bed and talk
about our day
or week
or really nothing at all.
Your hands are very rough
as you rub my back.
That means you put in a lot of perms
this week,
the chemicals
eating away at your skin
as you stand all day
on tired feet.
Ready for sleep
you pull the covers
over your head,
I put my bony little-kid knees
in your back
against your ribs.
As we drift off to sleep
it starts to rain
and a train rumbles
on the tracks
across the road.

Roaring away across the road the freight train passes – a hundred cars click-clack click-clack click-clack click-clack over and over and over – so many trains over the years they no longer wake us – four generations in this house have heard these trains – four generations have slept through them.

Rain pounds against the roof – somehow the moonlight still manages to softly illumine the room – I hear you breathing even under the covers – you, the train, the rain, the dark – it's safety – for the rest of my life few things take me back home like that combination.

For the Old Man Outside the Resort *by Sarah E. Morin*

I share the view
with only one other this morning.

The old man is already outside the resort.
The vacationers and honeymooners still drowse inside
tangled in blankets of each other.
Even the damp picnic tables are still asleep.
Perhaps they dream of romantic basket lunches long past:
croissants and sweet pungent wine,
French cheeses with names
the tongue learns to pronounce with awkward delight.

We're strangers so I claim another table.
But the old man has one of those faces you glance in every hometown
behind newspapers at the pancake joint.

We both bring books
but do not read them.
The sheets of paper are stained
with pale pink light.
The lamp of the world
can't rouse itself out of its rosy bed of clouds.

He sips sunrise from his coffee mug
but mostly cradles the chipped ceramic in veiny hands.
It's not the monogrammed foam kind
the hotel provides,
but I notice he's stolen their sugar packets.
White ghosts of creamer swirl and dissipate.

Should I say hello?
Interrupt the grass with dewy footprints?
But the dawn is a solemn Communion.
I want to ask him what he's reading/not reading,
but mainly why he brought
two cups.

An Extra Hour *by David Allen*

If I had an extra hour to spend
I'd spend it with my Muse
for we have lost children, words,
to tend and find them a line or two.
For there are many orphaned words,
more than an abandoned few,
left by the mind's blindside when
we wrapped up a final stanza for
poem famished friends to view.

untitled 1 *by John A. Caviness*

lush grass in winter
cold rain in mid-July heat
renewal in view

Golden Field 1 *by Sarah E. Morin*

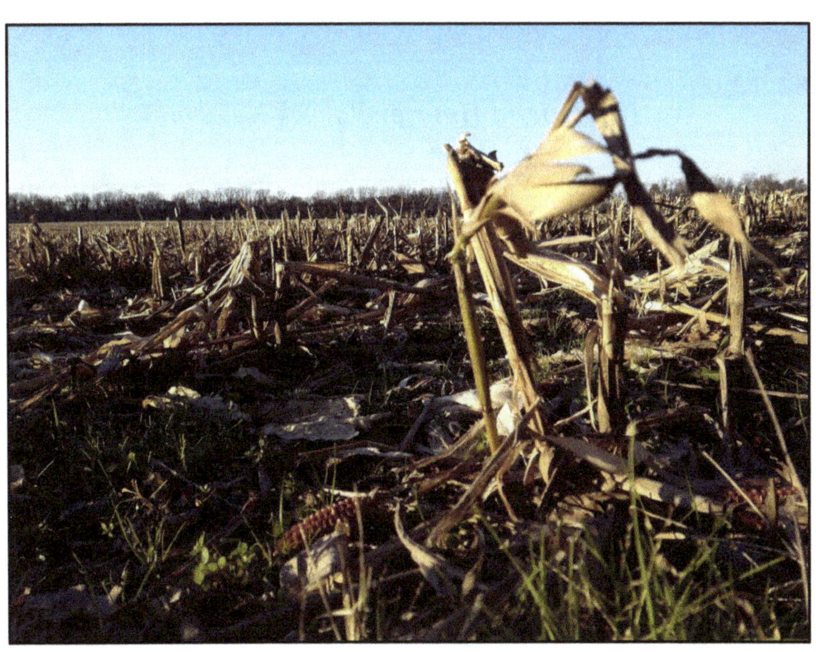

Retirement *by George W. Wolfe*

Is it not employment enough to watch the changing of the seasons?
– Henry David Thoreau

I keep trying to watch the seasons change, but I still get bored – keep looking for work, something meaningful to pour my residue ambition into, hoping it will erase the guilt of idleness that remains. So I've become a pilgrim on my personal Hajj to make peace with the natural world, traveling to that remote glacial park where I am challenged by cryogenic earth. I climb mountains graced in cloud negligees that were once in my fantasies, marvel at her frozen veins crushing granite with her bare hands. We hike the divide, negotiating the continental rift, a long division with quadratic quartz transformed into treasure, gems pressed into her crown. I seek to reconcile with mountain goats grazing along breath-robbing trails. We later take refuge in the lowlands amidst silent cedars, and meditate beside Lake MacDonald where once again I try watching the seasons change.

Glacier National Park
the "Crown of the Continent"
August, 2016

The Fateful Hour *by Patrick Kalahar* 

I first saw him in Battery Park in the summer of 1970. He was leaning at a precarious angle against the painted steel rails that were his only hindrance to a watery death in New York Harbor. The Statue of Liberty stood directly behind him – an incongruous backdrop to the drunken rant the man was delivering against Marshal Josip Broz Tito, Yugoslav President for Life.

He wore an old suit over a dingy white shirt, open at the collar. He had a beer bottle in one hand and a lit cigarette in the other, both of which he waved around furiously. Listening to him, I thought of Ben Franklin and Lenny Bruce at his most anti-religious and most profane – very astute and very much to the point.

I always wanted to be a writer, so I collected people the way someone else might collect rocks or keep a list of bird sightings. People who were weird or eccentric or plain crazy were the subjects of my hunt. I didn't want to make fun of them or mock them – never that – but I also didn't see them as people with their own joys or sorrows and their own triumphs as well as failures. I never thought about them as somebody's son or daughter, or as children running and playing in open fields or working on farms or negotiating the mean and dirty streets of a big city slum. To me, they were characters in a story.

All that changed that day in Battery Park. When the man stopped talking, and the small crowd that gathered to stare had walked away, I went up to him and asked him his name and why he hated Tito so much.

The man leaned toward me and pinned me with his eyes. His look was much more sly than drunk. Then he smiled, slightly shook his head, and placed his fingers – nicotine-stained and ingrained with dirt, along the side of his nose. He tapped there, saying, "Nobody knows, but Mijo knows."

"Tell me why you hate Tito. I *really* want to know."

"Nobody knows, but Mijo knows."

"So *tell* me."

His eyes looked away from mine and seemed to refocus on something distant in both time and place. "I knew him. Tito. Only he wasn't called Tito then. Just plain Josip. Josip Broz. Not from any of the mountain villages in our area . . . further away. We were all fighting the Nazis. I was told the word in English for what we were – 'partisans' . . . . Somebody in Belgrade sent Josip Broz to organize us against the Nazis. Josip was a Communist. The rest of us were plain mountain villagers trying to get rid of the Germans and protect our homes and families, but Josip had other plans. He had ambitions."

Then there was a long silence. Mijo was far away in his thoughts. Abruptly he said, "Let's get some beer. I know a place quite close. You're buying."

I said, "Of course."

The bar was the kind of place that was familiar in every seaport in the world – sawdust on the floor and smelling of urine, stale beer, and danger.

Mijo went up to the bar with the ten-dollar bill I had given him and came back with eight bottles on a battered tray. He didn't offer me any change. He lined up the eight bottles in front of him like a row of soldiers on parade and opened one, then he made a vague gesture toward the row and said, "Have one."

I opened a bottle, and Mijo began talking. Again, he abruptly changed the subject to his coming to America aboard a freighter and jumping ship in New York. He said he'd worked almost twenty-five years as a garbage man, about the only job he could get without papers.

He told of the grease and grime and filth he could never get out of his pores or the loops and whorls of his fingers – only he called them the pits and wrinkles in his skin. He told of finding dead animals in the garbage, and of many things far worse that even he couldn't say out loud. He told of being nearly killed when a garbage truck backed over him and of escaping a gang fight by jumping into a full dumpster head-first.

"It's strange … ever since the war, I've wanted to die. I should have died in the war with my comrades, but I didn't. I couldn't kill myself. It's my religion, you see. I wanted God to kill me, but every time He tried, I escaped. I'm cursed – cursed to live."

"But what about Tito and your dead comrades? What about the war? Why do you think you're cursed?"

Mijo looked down at the seven dead bottles lying on their side (mine was still upright in front of me) and said, "Let's have some more beer. I'm awfully dry from so much talking."

"I'm out of money."

Mijo said, "No matter. I have some."

I smiled. "Of course, you do."

The bottles were lined up the same as before, and Mijo began talking as if the last twenty-five years had never been mentioned.

"As I was saying, we only wanted to protect our homes and families, but Tito was ambitious and had other plans, as did the Communists in Belgrade. There was to be a large-scale raid on a German fortified encampment that informants had told us contained food, medicine, and guns and ammunition. It was to take place in three days, when there was no moon, and I was to lead because Tito was suddenly called to Belgrade, supposedly for new plans and instructions. I said we didn't have enough men for such a large-scale attack, and I would try to recruit more men in the surrounding villages, though I knew there were only women and older men and a few boys under eighteen. Everyone else was already fighting or in hiding. Many women were already fighting, but not in our area, and I knew it was time to ask that everybody fight.

"There was no way that new recruits would be gathered in time, let alone ready for battle. So, I headed back to the caves where my comrades were waiting, ahead of the recruits. I had to lead the raid that very night. I was almost back when I was captured by a German patrol. I pretended to be a simple farmer, very stupid and very cowardly, who had been in hiding. The German patrol didn't know what to do with me without orders. Shoot me as a spy or torture me for information. In the end, they did nothing but tie me up and hold me till they could hand me to someone with more authority. I was in a panic. I had to get back to lead the raid. Torture or death was nothing compared to letting down my comrades or being thought of as a coward and deserter. I had to get free – or die trying. Tied up like a pig, I managed to roll over, rise onto my knees, and beg to use the latrine or I would soil myself and their tent.

"They laughed at me, and I said I was a sorry excuse for a man, a coward and a weakling. But they cut the rope around my legs, and one of the soldiers led me out to a field and told me to dig my own hole. I said, 'I can't with my hands tied.' The guard just sneered, but he untied my hands. I started to dig a few shovels full, then threw a shovel of dirt in his face. When his hands went to his eyes, I hit him in the head with the flat of the shovel, and he went down. Then, I hit him with the edge, and that was that. I grabbed the guard's gun and knife and ran into the forest. Now, there was no time to go to our hideout in the cave. I had to go directly to the German fortified camp. It was a long and difficult way, avoiding roads and main trails. When I got there, the Germans were gone, and all our men were dead. It was treason, a betrayal, a carefully planned ambush, and it could only have been done by me or Tito, and I knew it wasn't me, but I couldn't prove it. I was supposed to lead, but I wasn't there. I was an hour too late. Some would say it was a gift of an hour because I survived, but to me, it was God's curse to have to live branded a traitor. I got to the Dalmatian coast and joined a crew of smugglers going to Spain and across land to Portugal and then signed on to a freighter going to America, where I jumped ship. The rest of my story, you already know. My whole life was cursed by a single hour when I should have died.

"Now I want to die in my homeland and drink beer and denounce Tito every day and tell everyone of his crimes. Maybe the Political Officer on the ship will kill me and say I fell overboard when I was drunk, but I don't think so. There would be too many questions. They will wait till I'm back home, and the Secret Police will arrest me. Maybe Tito will kill me himself. I was the only survivor of his betrayal – Tito should complete his work."

I left Mijo at the bar. I didn't know what to say, so silently, I wished him peace. After that day, I never collected people as characters. I only collected stories of the magic and strangeness of the human condition.

untitled; a senryū *by Marilyn J Wolf*

the box is fuller
than she wanted it to be
more to leave behind

Spent *by Paul "Spike" Wilson*

If time is money, is money time?
No, so many immeasurable things –
another hour with my father,
the first moments looking
in my new bride's eyes,
a day spent young, with noiseless promise.
But the truth
undercuts this fantasy: I
am not so much afraid of death as time.

untitled 2 *by Z. Rose*

working overtime counts up
as time counts down

but the future is unknowing
what time we put in
time is a concept made up
we gift ourselves time
an hour here
five minutes there
but it means nothing
only what you value in an hour
a glass of red wine
poured for more, but they ran out of time

buzzed and buried
left without a watch
remembered
in the gift of an hour

People, Please Pour In Some Adoration and Awe *by Ndaba Sibanda*

I cherish the magic of words that shows a reader
how I am in love with trees, sunsets, and sunrises,
poetry is my potent love and my labor of love,
yet people say poetry is one of the most
uncelebrated and underfunded art forms,
a pull-down poetry syndrome does not
in any way mean I am not enamoured
of poetry and its power and its role in life,
for without poetry how would I sing, swim
in the ecstasy of the wild and nature?
For without poetry how would I hear
the voices of the deeps, brooks, birds?
How would I explore the landscapes,
the human condition, the weather
patterns, the finery, controversies
and complexities of life?
Poetry, I pardon humans,
I am here to bare realities
for, I think, they err
on fostering fairness

as they fail to give
you what you merit!

Lovely, lively, fathomable, fun poetry,
please pave the way for the perfect pour
of my thoughts, blood, and emotions
so that I may not long to escape
the insanity that rules and marks
your words, world and wisdom
and call them a misplaced family
for in your oddness and boldness
is my safety, soundness, and sanity,
and where I see the world through
the prism of probe and preparation,
products that baptize me with visions
and hence it's my superb, stable family!
Please profound, philosophical poetry
bond me with your voltage and verve,
protect me with your prime punch –
your profundity, power, and precision,
bond me in a bold and intense fashion
as I savor each page of your digest and devour
each word, each sound, each line, and each stanza,
allow me to unwrap your splendor which empowers me
to capture all the magic and wonder of your ageless urgings,
let me seize my hot and much-loved cup of Ethiopian tea
and nestle under a comfy blanket and be transported afar!

America She's Cryin *by Kathy Bell and Bob McGilpin*
(song lyric)

What's happened to America she used to be so strong
The things that she's now seeing they are so very wrong
Her people need to stand together and put up a good fight
Her morals and her constitution have been compromised

America's seeing many things she never thought she'd see
Now she is a wondering who will her next leader be
Will they be corrupt or will they keep our country free

Only time will tell and we'll just have to wait and see

America she's cryin, Keep standing tall let's give all we've got
America she's cryin, Let's take our country back cause we the people are the boss
It's time for us as a nation to finally say enough is enough
America she's cryin, Have some backbone, stand together even when the times get tough

America is wondering what will happen next
Can she survive the hard times as she faces many tests
It's time now as a nation we take some time today
To know in God we trust as we bow our heads and pray

America she's cryin, Keep standing tall let's give all we've got
America she's cryin, Let's take our country back cause we the people are the boss
It's time for us as a nation to finally say enough is enough
America she's cryin, Have some backbone, stand together even when the times get tough

It's only with God's help that we can turn this around
If we follow him he'll put us back on solid ground
God will one day show us we have nothing to fear
When we place our faith in him, he'll dry every tear

America she's cryin, Keep standing tall let's give all we've got
America she's cryin, Let's take our country back cause we the people are the boss
It's time for us as a nation to finally say enough is enough
America she's cryin, Have some backbone, stand together even when the times get tough

America she's cryin
America she's cryin,
America she's cryin,
America she's cryin
Oh stop your crying

Date Night Sunrise *by Sarah E. Morin*

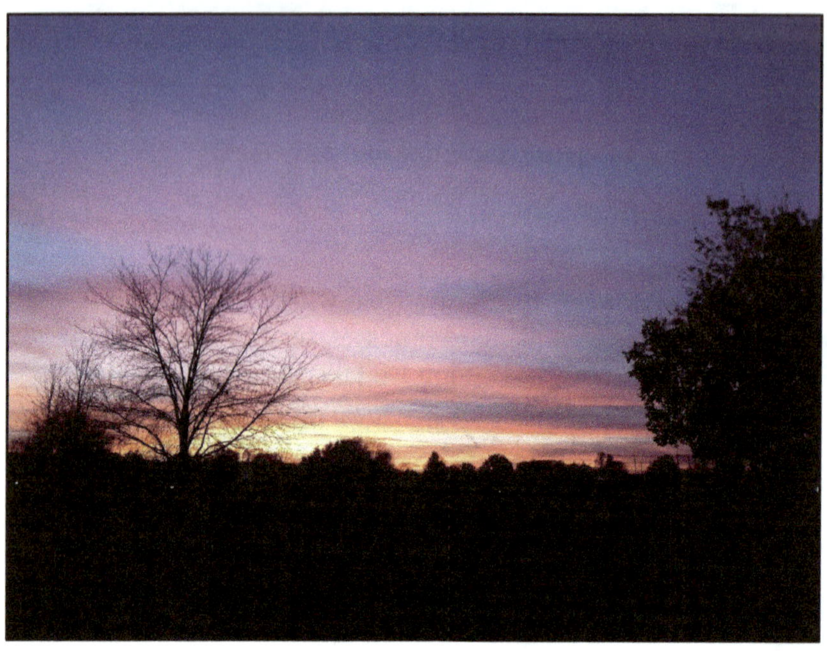

Verses Re-Versus no. 13 *by George W. Wolfe* 

Author's note: the second stanza of a Verses Re-Versus poem is the first stanza with the words written in reverse order.

Spirit . . . ailing, an echo within and
away, slipping time through twisted
seasons, endlessly calls us beneath
cracked and choking earth. Our eyes
roving with quietly placed steps, watch
clouds passing amidst grazing elk.

Elk grazing amidst passing clouds
watch steps placed quietly with roving
eyes. Our earth, choking and cracked
beneath us, calls endlessly. Seasons
twisted through time, slipping away
and within, echo an ailing spirit.

The Hour Passeth *by Vivianne Belle*

Say what you will,
the hour passeth.
It passeth despite desire
to stop the clock and
silence that never-ending
tick-tock.

It passeth, tho' you wish and try
to stem the reversed tide of
memories fading, or to combat
the dullness of stringing graying
past-bright hair,
and it passeth even tho' you struggle
to carry the heft of
ever-lumpier sagging flesh.

tick-tock

The hour passeth, taking its toll
upon body and mind,
and spirit confronts vicissitudes
violently whirling within and
without, for the hour passeth also
in the transforming world,
tho' you wish and try
to stop the Earth from turning.

tick-tock
the hour passeth inexorably
tick-tock

One grain of sand at a time,
dropping through a steadfast hourglass,
sanding away an infinity of hours.

tick-tock

Say what you will, still
in each grain of sand
exists eternity.

For Holly Middleton *by Kitty O'Doherty*

It could have been any one of about a dozen of us middle-school-aged kids who were living in the eastside Indianapolis apartment complex in late 1970, but it was Holly Middleton.

In the summer we'd all hang out at the pool, learning to swim, playing Marco Polo, getting Pepsi out of the vending machine, watching the teenagers doing their preening and working on their Indiana version of a Malibu tan. Come the frosty fall mornings, we would huddle together at the bus stop in the front of the complex, waking up and talking about homework, The Monkees, and our various blooming crushes.

Holly wasn't my best friend, but she was a good friend by virtue of our shared social proximity in the apartment complex. She was a year younger than I, and tall, but not the tallest of the kids. She was cute, very cute. So cute. Dark hair and laughed easily. She was fun. She was skinny and her knees were knobby. Sometimes she would bite her nails while she was listening to someone talk. I remember thinking that looked oddly adorable, so for about a week I tried biting my nails. I looked ridiculous. Only Holly could make nail-biting and knobby little knees adorable.

On the bus rides home from school we'd all be full of energy and the boys would be rowdy. Plans would be made for the time between homework and dinner to meet at the apartment playground or just walk around.

This one particular afternoon Holly went to the neighboring apartment of another girl, to hang out, do "girl" stuff. They probably planned to watch the popular late afternoon goth soap opera Dark Shadows and talk about everything twelve-year-olds talk about. Just like the rest of us were doing that December day.

I had never been to a funeral home before. It was the mother of a friend who took a car full of us to say a final goodbye to Holly.

The scene was so surreal. All of us kids were crying. Adults were crying. Holly was laying there in a white casket, our lifeless friend surrounded by beautiful flowers. I remember worrying about her little sister. How everything would be with no Holly in the friend circle. And most of all just how awful, awful, awful it was that the neighbor's brother brought a gun into the room where the girls were. Holly had died of an accidental shot to the chest. At twelve years old.

My family moved to the other side of town a month later and I have thought about Holly many times over the years. What would she have been like in high school or where would her life have taken her as an adult? She would be getting near retirement age now. Same as the rest of "us kids."

It has seemed somehow personally important to keep her memory alive. I didn't know her parents, nor really her sister, and if there had been any way to say, "Yes, I very much remember Holly," I would have loved to have given that to them at some point in the following years. To let them know their daughter, their sister, is remembered even decades later.

She was only twelve. It could have been any one of about a dozen of us junior-high-aged kids, but on that sad day it was Holly Middleton. And I have never forgotten her.

Preserved *by Patrick Kalahar*

Trying write on the subject of time,
I realize nearly all my poems are about time
in one way or another –
trying to capture the ephemeral moment,
the grains of our existence that together make a life,
trying to encase in amber or in iron
something as brief and fleeting
as the heartbeat of a hummingbird.

I often question if time even exists,
or if the universe began when I was born
and ceases when I die –
which, of course, it does.
But I read old books,
meet old portraits eye to eye,
listen to the last castrato sing a terrible lament
on a century-old recording,
so I know there are other lives,

other universes that overlap my own.
Maimonides said that in preserving a single life,
all life is preserved.
Perhaps if I can preserve a moment,
every moment might last forever somewhere
in a place called Time.

untitled 2 *by B. Monét*

standing hourglass
sand slipping through both my hands
trapped and forgotten

Please Purify And Placate My Soul *by Ndaba Sibanda* 

I recall when I asked you to be my juice,
elixir, honeybun, you said you are profuse

under the spell of your touch and scent
I did not comprehend what you meant

honeybun, you taught me what sunburn
is, honey, I love how you punch heartburn

let me unlock your feats, your benefits –
as laudable gels are your byproducts

we all seek to stay happy and hydrated
water-dense, you can't be underrated

you help us detox, purge, and flush out
impurities, as we take you after a workout

soothing like a careful, cool sweetheart
massaging like a caring, cleansing dearest
when one wants to keep the skin clear,
and hydrated, they take you without fear

you don't only heal burns, there is a wealth
of proof that you boost oral and digestive health

you excite me as you inspire peristalsis to help pass
stool without hurt or hassle, you are your own class!

natural laxative, go on fixing fissures, treating the skin
aloe vera, you patch up puffy gums, sunburn, heartburn

you come to our rescue when we are constipated
your nutrients and benefits leave us captivated

Winter Bridge *by Marilyn J Wolf*

Bridge looks like cement.
It's ice. Walking carefully.
Sun starts to melt it.

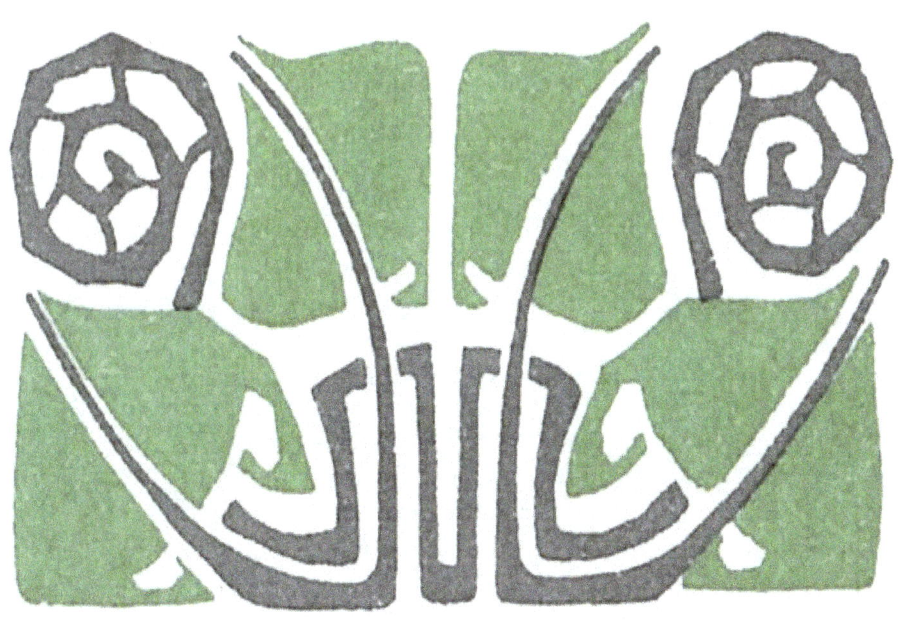

Ready for Festivities *by Sarah E. Morin*

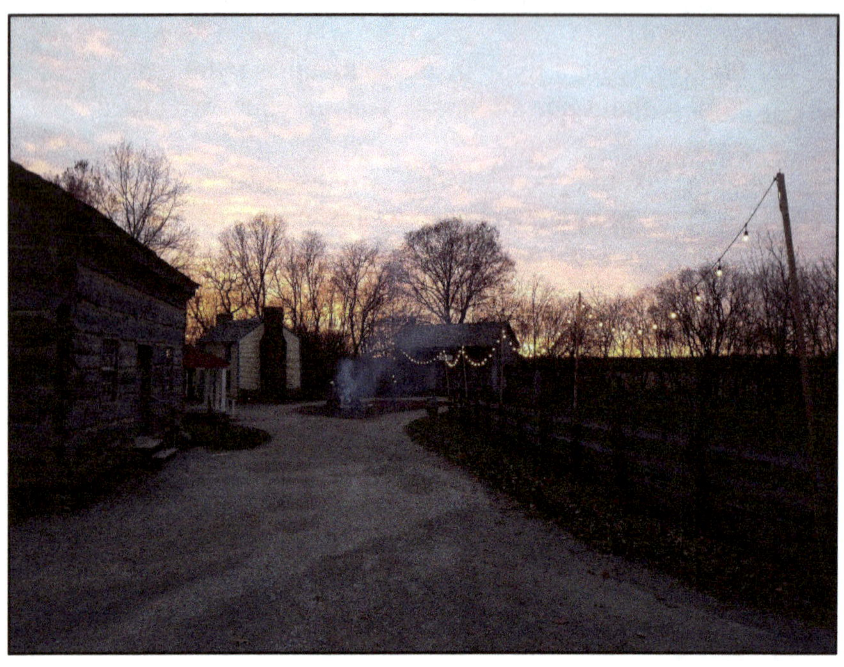

In An Hour *by Alys Caviness-Gober*

once, everything stopped
an hour of eternity
in broken embrace
like a headlong collision
wrapping me around a tree
life, as known, perished

Stay-at-Home Sheep *by Jenny Kalahar*

A lonely sheep through winter,
she is layered in wool of her own making,
uncombed, her sweatpants high over hips,
off-brand mulberry tea cooling on the couch-side table,
she complains to the dog that there is nothing on cable. Again.
Knitting is dull and dirty work
when the yarn drags through leavings in the cushions –

Frito fragments and breadcrumbs,
and some lint that may be the yellow dried-slobbery fuzz
from a tug toy that Bandit chewed to bits last year.

A lonely sheep through spring,
she sighs over the crossword puzzle
that is either too easy or too hard,
her own handwriting a lazy mess from disuse –
so many years typing at the office surely to blame.
Now stuck at home,
day after day, no end in sight,
sitting in on Zooms but not paying attention,
happy to be away from Doug in advertising
who kept complaining about his wife,
and away from Randy
who wouldn't stop following her
every time she went to the copy machine.
There are worse things
than working from home during pandemic times.

A lonely sheep through summer,
she peers around her curtains
at the neighbor being hauled out on a gurney,
red lights on the ambulance
beckoning kids in the park to rush over
to stare at Mr. Cooper in his white boxers and socks,
strapped down but still commanding,
giving orders to his shirtless son
about how often to mow the lawn while he's in the hospital.

There are worse things
than working from home during pandemic times.
You could have this plague.
You could find yourself surrounded at the grocery store
by a bunch of anti-maskers
who are aggressively giving you the evil eye
for trying to protect them from themselves.

A lonely sheep through autumn,
she steps to the couch,

grabs knitting needles,
pets the overweight dog at her side,
changes over to the Hallmark channel
for the start of an early Christmas moviethon.
She opens another bag of chips,
sighing a Covid-free sigh of stale household air,
determined to be content in confinement
until it's time to plant a victory garden again.

Snow on the Redbud *by Jean Roberts*

Being a description of
a late April snow, 2021

Snow on the wildflowers and on
the flowering trees
fat straight down flakes
turning the spreading purple redbud
to pale violet
a red cardinal, a black redwing blackbird
wait their turn
decorating the scene.

All the birds are gathering
in sequence as in verse.
Eat now! is their message
in case it gets worse.

All the birds are gathering
the woodpecker, the goldfinch,
and the dove
the redbud's hue grows increasing paler
its bark the darker black
the scene whiter the birds brighter.

Snow sheds down from above
it should go on for hours
finally the tree was reduced to black and white
a puffed-up wren calls from a sheltered spot

a great squirrel chase across the lawn
and into the woods beyond.

Competition under the feeder
between a little red squirrel
and a large gray squirrel
the little one drives the larger squirrel off
he also owns the spot *vs* a chipmunk
after many graceful skirmishes.

Snow turned finer and accumulated
here is the red squirrel running off a cardinal family
finally the dove family, like fat muffins, and
the larger, flowing squirrels.

An inch and a half of snow
a cardinal in a deep green arborvitae tree
with white snow topped branches
surveys the busy scene looking for his opportunity.

Two inches of snow
rotate again to my neighborhood birds,
the chickadee, the titmouse
doves, woodpecker, cardinal
they look so urgent and desperate
they ate it all by dark.

Two and a half inches of snow
it's still snowing and we are swamped in white
dusk settles after the seed is all consumed.
Three inches of snow
finally everything is covered in white
like icing over dark twiggy bark
more icing than cake.

This blue light of twilight that I have always loved
greenish tonight under these heavy clouds
and then the power went out.

Four haikus *by Patrick Kalahar*

a poet's stolen words
scrape their sad wings in the trees
the sound of locusts

glistening morning dew
on spiders' delicate webs
proclaim the Dawn

the tentative night
shocked by the dog's bark
fitfully returns to sleep

the sun-stroked cat
curls around the summer heat
dreaming of Lions

untitled 3 *by B. Monét*

lost in translation
spiraling out of control
time machine warped

untitled 2 *by John A. Caviness*

evening so noiseless
tempered coils on lush satin
bewildered in view

Untitled *by Sarah E. Morin*

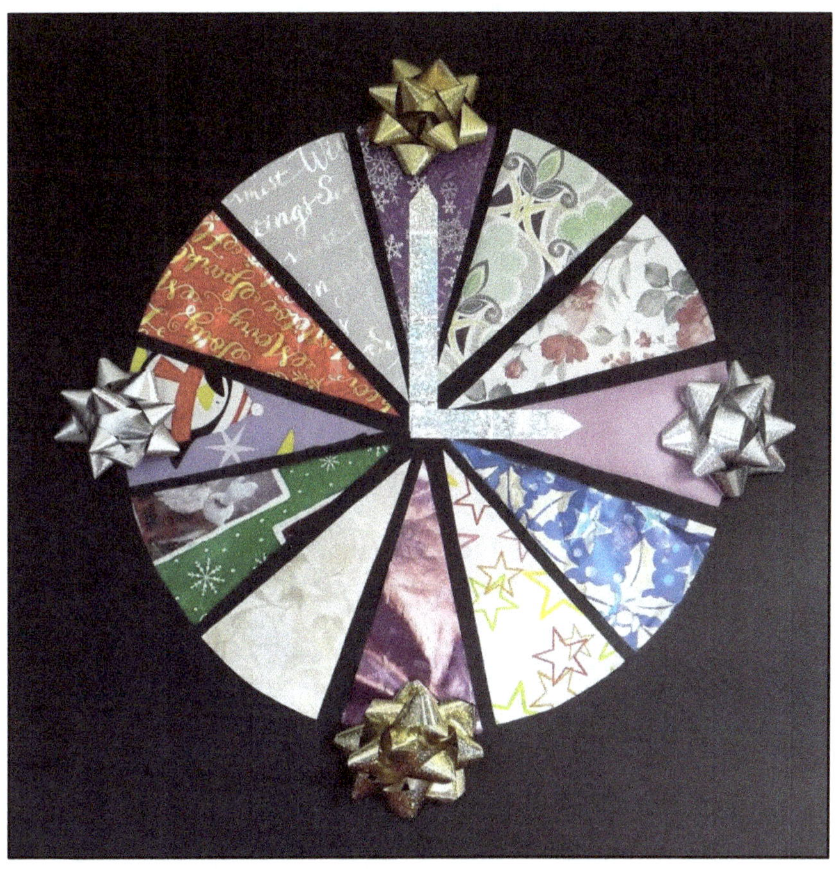

This piece is my on-the-nose interpretation of our 2022 theme, as I enjoy a good pun. It is also made of entirely repurposed gift wrapping, both from gifts I have given and gifts I have received. Assembling the piece brought back memories of those precious hours of many family celebrations. More valuable than the objects given, which I may or may not remember, is the time spent in togetherness.

untitled 3 *by Z. Rose*

meet me at this time
but the hour will blow by
free me from this loop

The Soft Snow Fell *by Alys Caviness-Gober*

The soft snow fell
from a hard grey sky,

floating

steadily down,
lingering gently
on every surface
like whispered words
of love.

Time And Time Again *by David Allen*

You want to know about time?
Well, time is of the essence.
Do you have the time?
Remember, time waits for no man
and Father Time at no time bides his time.
We all know there's no time like the present
and there's little time to waste.
So, hear me out this time,
'cause the time is ripe.
Anyway, if you just take the time
you'll realize there's a time
and place for everything.
And though the bad times
seem to always follow the good times,
at one time or another,
we all learn that only time will tell
if the third time really is the charm.
Just mull on this in your spare time,
time weighs heavy on this time of life.
But time can also work wonders,
even if you're living on borrowed time.
So, here's to you, this time.
I am wishing you a whale of a time,
hoping you're not wasting time

counting the seconds, minutes, and hours,
parsing your time,
getting lost in the mists of time,
until, at last, you run out of time
and finally realize time
is no longer on your side.
So, it's now just time
to call it a day, marking time
as we are all washed away.
in the sands of time.
Because time and tide
wait for no man.

Kindred Spirit *by Chuck Kellum*

Aren't we all
Searching
For kindred spirits?

The ones who
Already
Know how we
Feel, what we
Think, and
The things we
Want
And like
To do

Simply because
Despite all
Our many varied differences
In those ways
We are
The way
They are
Themselves.

Yesterday in Crawfordsville *by Kitty O'Doherty*

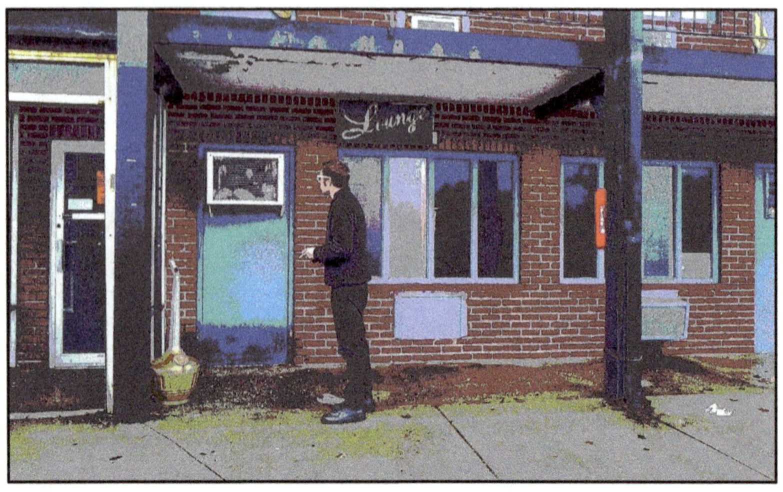

Musical Inspiration *by Marilyn J Wolf*

As the sun moves toward the horizon,
she turns to the meadow.
Her dress moves softly with the breeze
and highlights the movement of her thighs.
The grasses brush her knees
and tangle in the hem of her dress.
The light flows through her hair
as his fingers will no more.

Author's note:

I attended an online workshop on "Ekphrastic Writing with Music" presented by Kendra Preston Leonard. I really enjoyed it, and wrote this poem while listening to: Field, Hilary. 2015. "Donazella-Fantasia on a Sephardic Lullaby" On *Premieres*.
Ekphrastic; from the Greek, *Ekphrasis* [pr., eck-FRAY-ses], being a written description about a piece of art as a literary device, or a piece of writing inspired by a work of art.

Waiting *by David Allen*

The hour delay
in releasing
the patient
taught the
non-patients
patience.

(untitled haiku/senryū) *by Chuck Kellum*

Daylight Savings Time

Gives and takes an hour each way

Sun and moon don't care

Anima's Dream *by Kristine Staley*

This painting is a fun representation of a female dreamer who loves floral shapes and may be thinking about next year's garden. What flowers will she plant? What are the colors and shapes she would like to see? Anima should also be pursuing a Master Gardener Certificate, which several of her friends have already earned.

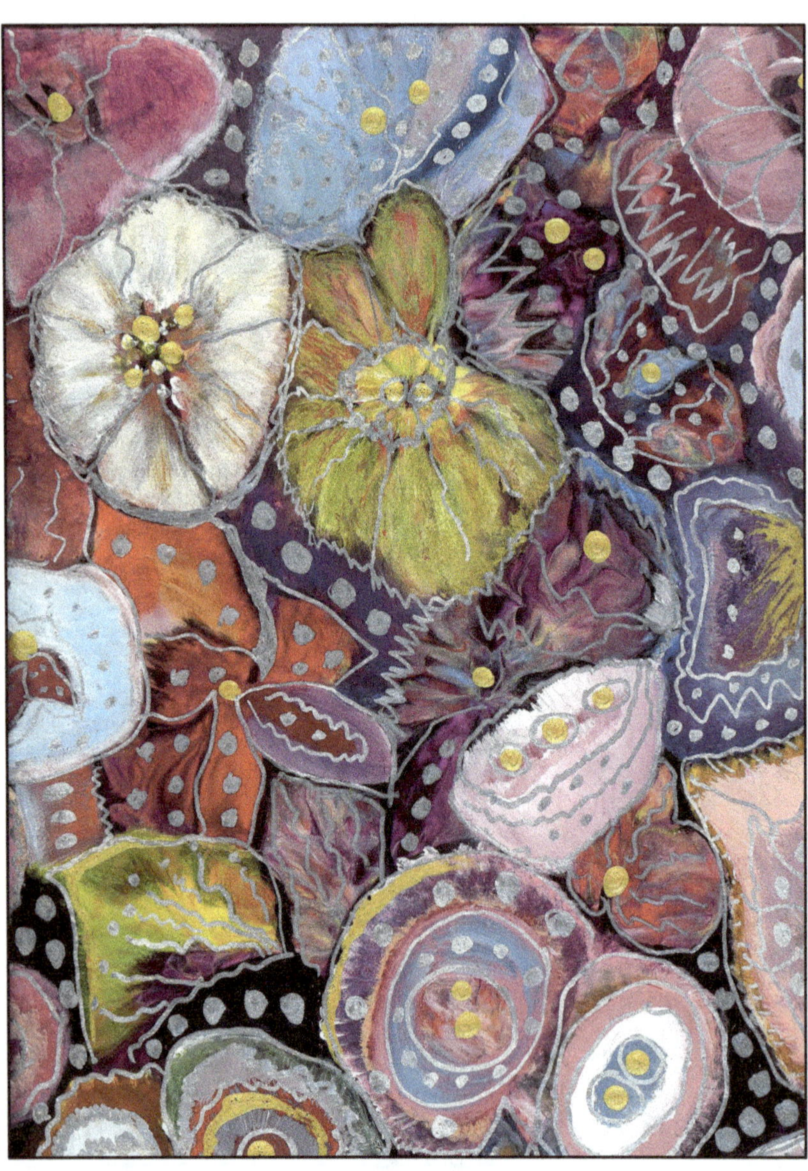

untitled 3 *by John A. Caviness*

coarse grains always stand
travel flecked in collision
unremoved despite

Pandemic Fever Dreams – Paradise *by Patrick Kalahar* 

Nature is branded now. On Walden Pond
the lilies are multicolored bottlecaps,
and the water comes from Pure Icelandic Glaciers

with effervescence added from gasses
of slowly decaying corpses of Pre-Adamites
caught in the first Age of Ice.

The frogs are tattooed with trademarks
and wear body lotion scented with extinct extracts
to "protect that alluring and desirable sheen."
The fish are articulated with paperclips
and held in place with string.
They look to the commercial-filled sky
with eyes of recycled glass.

On the Hallmark shore, pines are decorated
with Keepsake ornaments and stenciled with
rhyming verses sprayed on with an aerosol can.

Beetles scurry with frenzied purpose on wheels
instead of legs, compliments of Adolf Hitler
and Dr. Ferdinand Porsche.

In the cities, advertising is the only art,
and mankind is manufactured,
fully programmed and wired for sound.

GPS implants can locate everyone
within three feet of reality and
chart the temperature of their thoughts.

No one works. This is Paradise
and money has been abolished. Credits and

demerits received by phone and stored
in the cloud determine their future.

Our job is to consume and consume.
As for living, our robots will do that for us.
We have more important things to do.

We have our sacred religion.
Three times a day we are called to prayer.
Around the world there are:

seven thousand thousand phallic towers
known as the Pillars of Wisdom. On them is
inscribed all the knowledge of the Universe,
written in a long-forgotten language.

In diabolic formation with ecstatic eyes
and glistening and hairless bodies,
we goosestep around them.

Sometimes we march to the Right,
following the turn of the Earth.
Sometimes we march to the Left,
following the retreat of the sun.

Sometimes half goes Right and half Left,
and chaos and carnage ensue,
but it diminishes the surplus population,

the Final Solution in our perfect world.
In our Paradise, everlasting
sleep is the only cure for dreaming.

A Pretty Prodigy From Binga *by Ndaba Sibanda* 

she had been written
off by prophets of doom
who define and confine
one based on their whims

hailing from deep down
in Binga, rustic and poor,

the diviners of disasters
looked down upon her

but professors professed
that her sharpness was
on a raised, rare podium,
an acuteness's stadium,
and her accessories and
clothing were intuitions

on a rump, Ntombi cruised
and danced and devoured
a feast of words, a fashion
show of figures and facts

a studious student studied
like a supermodel catwalking
to high acclaim on a walkway
of elegance and intelligence,
her confidence conferred rays
of sunshine, polish, and poise

on the pages of assignments,
exams and heavy cogitations,
she shamed scholarly schemes
and hypnotized her professors

untitled 4 *by Z. Rose*

secrets seep through me
still believe my perspective
swapped back at sight

When Winter Steals My Colors *by Jenny Kalahar*

Blueness seeps from my eyes tonight;
red leaks from my pumping heart into a spill.
Whiteness settles among the roots at my forehead,
and black noise congests these straining ears.

Colors hurt. Lack of color, even more.
It pains me when fragile pigments burst.
My birthmark melts from wrist to fingers,
permanently inking all I touch.
These lips long for scorching kisses,
tough and tender both
to paint them pink again.
Eyes in winter forget rainbows exist.
All is dull, sharply gray, black and white.

When spring stops teasing and returns,
I'll reach higher than I ever have
to steal blueness from the sky,
borrow redness from a startled robin's breast,
dye my hair in whatever thawed pond I can find.
With only the snapping sounds of breaking buds
and the heavy flaps of owls
as they swoop brownly from barn lofts,
I'll see clearer, farther, truer
without the crusting, muting blankets of ice and sin
covering everything.

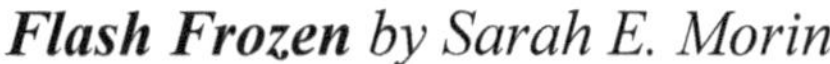

Flash Frozen *by Sarah E. Morin*

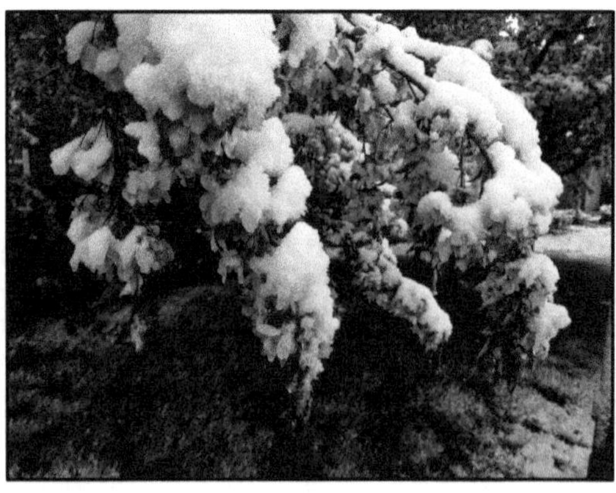

Gramma's World *by George W. Wolfe*
(for Della Walter, in memoriam)

The railroad tracks lie rusted,
winding beneath thistles and chicory
as if looking for a destination,
or an escape from the place where
Gramma lived, still caring for the
house tucked away in what memory
was left, and for her five surviving
children who were old enough
to watch her mind wilt away. I was too
young to understand the time she
mistook my kite for a tablecloth.
Gramma's world was different than ours.

She enjoyed our Sunday drives through
the changing seasons, the family
picnics amidst mountain laurel, until
the day we left her behind hospital
doors. Soon our visits became
routine. Each time we'd call to her,
trying to find a passage into her
prison, or move our mental screens into
her line of focus, knowing her
heart still spoke its silent language.

I'd smile when we'd say goodbye,
praying that she knew me.

Poet Laureate Consultant Of Mthwakazi *by Ndaba Sibanda* 

I had shrunk in the noises of a slighting silence,
However, when the King of Mthwakazi appeared,
he pointed at the sun and its rays regally poured on me
like a shower, and I started to feel at home and honored;
He also pointed at a cute clock and an array of chiefs.

There was a constellation of stars, like local
footballers, movie directors, socialites, authors,

educators, and motivators. There was a galaxy of award-winning actors, sportspersons, and journalists. I saw icons and great thinkers. What remarkable talents!

There was a throng of human rightists, a bench of uncaptured judges, a flock of religious folks, and culturists. There was a diaspora of people who worked and lived in South Africa, Botswana, Namibia, Australia , US, UK, New Zealand, and several different parts of the world.

There was a regiment of activists, there was a swarm of feminists and legislators. There was a troop of soldiers and there was a wave of police officers. There was a huddle of elderly women and men, and a busload of singers and dancers. Indeed, there was a lovely troupe of entertainers.

There was a band of musicians that belted out divine music. The King showed me a host of editors and readers who were keenly watching the proceedings virtually, waving at us. On Zoom, I saw the new Mayor of Bulawayo, she was waving at me with her assemblage of excited, charismatic councilors.

I saw eminent radio and TV personalities, TV script writers, and famous playwrights. The King was moving around with me, with his entourage of advisors and security personnel, and a legion of diplomats and officials from neighboring countries. I caught sight of a nexus of my family members and relatives. I was speechless.

Some women wore headbands, thick knee-length cow-hide skirts or short skirts made of grass or beaded cotton strings, necklaces, beaded high heels or cute crochet sandals or beaded sandals, yet men wore animal skins and feathers, clusters of a cow's tail on the upper arm and underneath the knee, rubber batata sandals.

"There's a mass of people from all walks of life, there's a multitude. This is a momentous occasion. All these people have gathered here to honor you. Yes, *you*," emphasized the King, who wore ostrich feathers, a leopard skin, a front apron, and a rear apron or *ibhetshu.* He talked about the restoration of values and dignity.
I was stunned and confused. The cheerful, revered, and good-looking King took me on a tour along Nkululeko road until we marched into an august building.

"This is our parliament," said the King, as I admired the scent emanating from an entrance draped in a variety of superb trees and flowers. What a parliamentary chamber, what a monument.

I marveled at its design. The architecture had a traditional touch to it with a spear-shaped ceiling that shimmered with 30,000 aluminum panels. Its interiors were simple, yet colorful, delightful, and powerful. The circular space adorned with the statues of King Mzilikazi and King Mambo, signified the history of a new nation.

The King continued, "Piker Press calls you a Prophet of Liberation. Do you have a pen name? Do you sometimes publish under a different name?" I responded promptly, "Bhija Jamela. I inherited that name from my grandpa." He smiled, "Great. We're gathered here to appoint you as an officer of the royal household. As the Poet Laureate of Mthwakazi, you'll promote the reading and writing of poetry nationally." *What a vision*!

Surprise Rainbow *by Sarah E. Morin*

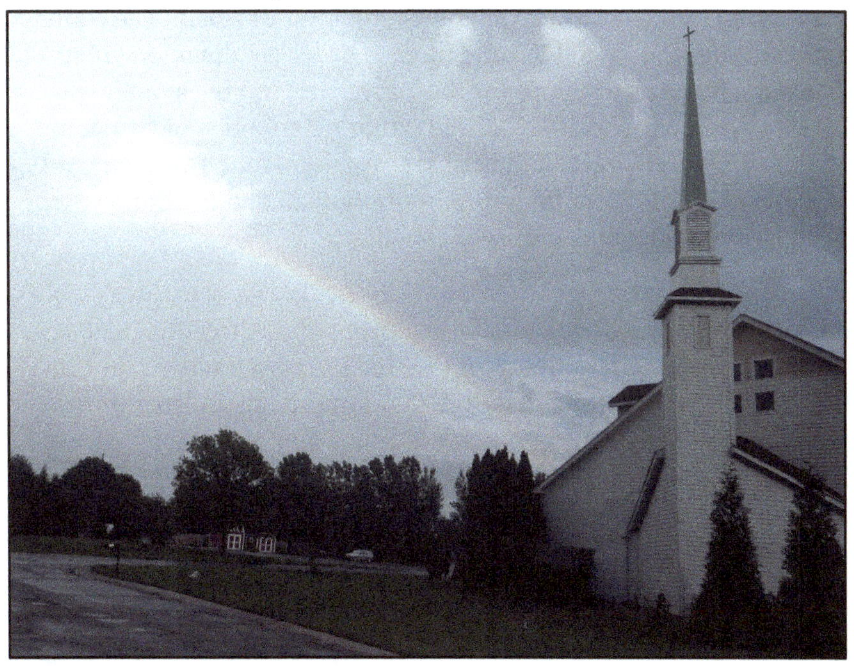

Oak Strength *by Gail Mehlan* 

A shoot will come up from the stump of Jesse; from its roots a Branch will bear fruit.

The Spirit of the Lord will rest on him . . .
The Spirit of wisdom and understanding,
The Spirit of counsel and power,
The Spirit of knowledge and fear of the Lord . . .

– Isaiah 11:1-2

My neighbor has an enormous oak tree in her backyard. It stands majestically above all the trees and the houses in our two yards. It is a beautiful tree with long twisted branches and today, sun filtering through it, its orange-tinged leaves made a beautiful glow in the sunlight. Several of its young saplings are growing in our yard. Even though they have sprouted where we don't want them, we guard each one carefully, hoping that we can transplant them as they begin to grow larger. Looking at this tree made me think of an oak tree we saw on our recent trip to Spain.

In May, we visited the small town of Guernika, Spain. This town was made famous by a life-altering and pivotal battle that took place during the Spanish Civil War in 1937. Franco, dictator of Spain, had violated the rules of neutrality and asked Hitler to order an attack on Guernika, the center of the government for the Basque region in Spain, using incendiary bombs. The attack killed children, animals, older people, and almost all civilians. The intent was to kill off the Basque people, and they nearly did. The famous Assembly Hall and the old oak tree were the only things that survived the attack.

We were able to visit the Assembly Hall the day we were there and were blessed to see the remains of the original oak tree that had survived the attack. The stump of the tree remains a sacred spot in Guernika. There is another oak tree that now stands in front of the Assembly Hall. It is the *"hijo del hijo"* the "son of the son", grown from a small acorn that had dropped from the original tree. This acorn grew into a large oak and when the original tree died it replaced the original tree.

The tradition of the Basque communities at the Assembly Hall was that all important "agreements" were always made under that old oak tree. Under this oak, laws were made, treaties signed, marriages took place, and delegates from all across Spain would come to settle disagreements. The tree witnessed many decisions made there with wisdom and understanding, counsel and power and faith. The tradition carries on.

I like the idea of the oak tree . . . strong and ancient, a symbol of sturdiness and refuge in a time of war, withstanding an attack and living through it to produce acorns that grew themselves into great sprawling trees as well. Survivors, who continued in their strength to produce and grow into the next generation of oaks. Underneath the oak is a good place to take an oath or make a promise that will *sobrevivir, (Which literally translated means "live above")* to carry forward the good, healthy and life-giving strength of the oak tree.

As I looked at that oak tree this morning, I remembered the oak of Guernika, and also thought of the stump of Jesse . . . growing . . . bearing fruit. We don't know what will grow from a tiny acorn. Certainly it will be an unexpected miracle. I call it oak strength. I want to hold onto the idea of "oak strength" as something important I can pass on in small little ways, "acorn" ways, to my grandchildren. Oak strength is spiritual strength.

***Echoes** by Alys Caviness-Gober*

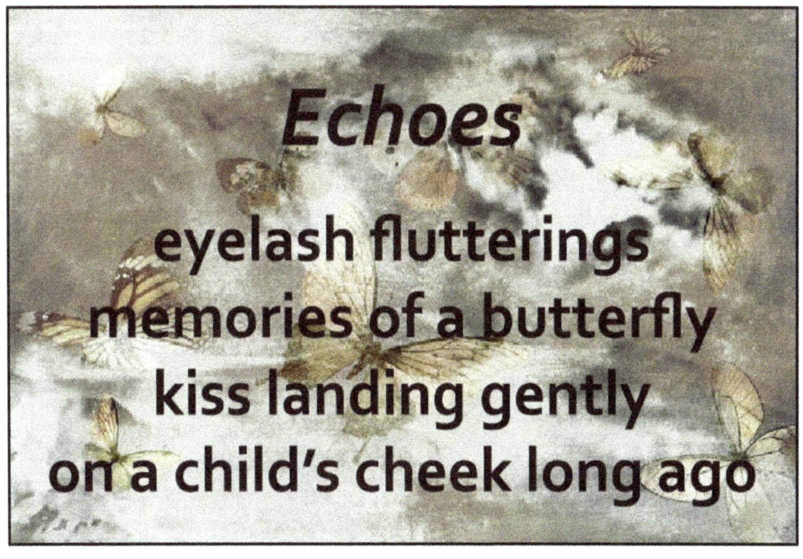

Adjusting Trajectories *by Nancy Simmonds*

The red bird huddles on a hoar frosted rafter
as winter winds whistle like a train through Potter's Bridge.
Bitter cold and white, the bridge, the wind
barrels through the open windowed span dragging icicle

ribbons of New Year's Resolutions in its wake.
'Precision' races over and around, through the bridge,
taking the lead and gone, hugging the river water's shore
with an inch to spare. The bold ribbon is a song

humming with the rhythm of bicycle tires on the wooden
bridge's floor: flippety pat, flippety pat, 'Imagine that!'
Mittened boys in winter coats brave the ice lined trails
while bare limbed trees clatchet overhead. A hat snatching

gust of arctic air blasts by as the siren song of success
whaps them upside the head. Busy living, busy 'Being'
they pedal out and away, away. Out the second window
on the left 'Relentless Incrementalism' dives clean

and crisp into The White then geysers the winking waters
like a giggling bubbler blowing snow globes etched
with broad, deep, accumulating designs of happiness.
A bundled hiker striding through cobwebs watches, listens, pauses,

adjusts a trajectory as the wind whispers Yes. Yes. Yes.
Attend! Heed that cold and watchful bird blinking bright and bold
as he shivers and halloos his accompaniment to the possibilities
stirring, soaring, here for the grasping any day of this new year.

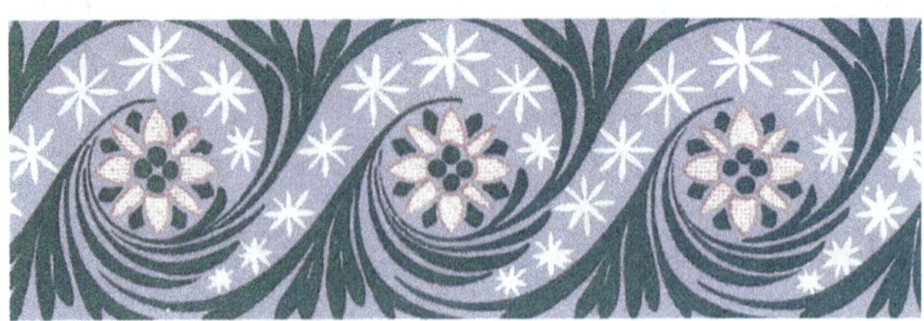

Editors' note: CEArts encourages the use of inclusive language. As editors, it is sometimes hard to strike a balance between artistic freedom and the most current inclusive terminology when referring to history and marginalized groups. In pieces that we publish, whether fiction or based on historical fact, we have chosen to let some period terminology stand, even if those terms have been updated in popular culture to reflect the evolution of language and more inclusive practices.

Resilience *by Gail Mehlan*

(written about Frances Adams Norris Parker,
30 January 1926 – 16 January 2021)

In my imagination . . .
I am a small girl
standing in the kitchen,
wiping sleep from my eyes.
I see the dog, Jigs, running into the house
tail wagging, tags jingling.
The dog barks yearningly.
Mother shouts at one of the farm workers,
        "Go look for Walter, please!"
I see Mother standing at the sink.
There is a far-away look on her face.
I snuggle up to her and hug her legs . . . what is wrong?
Suddenly a colored worker
comes running through the door
seeking help.
Rustling feet,
whispers so I can't hear
        "Go get Robert, we need help . . . "
A few minutes pass,
I hear the dog . . . continuing to bark, beckoning.
More people arrive,
more shuffling,
more whispering,
then quiet.

I'm playing on the floor
with my dolly and books.
Looking up, I see Mother

standing in the doorway.
Morning light surrounding
her figure there,
head leaning against the frame.
A tear falls from her eyes
as Jigs runs through the door again . . .
        "Walter is gone, shot himself in the heart."
I hear them whisper as my uncle touches
my mother gently on the back.
        "Where's daddy?" I ask
in my imagination.

Resilience #2 *by Gail Mehlan*

I asked her one afternoon, "What are you the most excited about learning when you get to heaven, Mom?"

"I don't know – I have always wondered why my dad killed himself. I'd really like to ask him why – and talk to him about it."

"Me too," I said casually, yet I sympathize. "I wonder about that too."

This conversation came back to me just the other day as I sat looking for clues about her family's genealogy. Who was who? How were they all connected? Why did they do what they did? I'm so fortunate that my mom lived until almost 95. I was able to speak with her often, and I always asked questions about some of these experiences. But the wondering about this particular story still haunts me and nearly breaks my heart. She was so very young when it happened. As I'm researching the family history online, a death certificate pops up on my computer screen. I see the old-fashioned handwriting on the right-hand side of the document that says boldly and seemingly without feeling, *Cause of death: Suicide by gunshot.*

I'm working on writing the family stories, and immediately as I see this information open up in front of me, it all seems so complicated and so deeply personal. Oh, I'd heard the story before. None of it was ever really a secret. It just startled me when I saw the words so boldly printed on the page. I began to think about my mother as a very young, small child riding on a tricycle in one picture and happily riding in a carriage with a big black dog in another with carefully printed words on the edge of the page in faded ink, "She loves to ride!"

The clock and calendar in my head begin to roll backward, and I begin to feel like I was there with the family as this story unfolded. I think about my mother, who lived such a full and loving life. No one would ever have known that these horrible events occurred in her early years. Still, I wonder, not so much about all the details, but about this; What about her life after all this made her grow into the gracious, resilient, loving mother and grandmother that she was? What course did her life take that healed her small 3-year-old heart and kept her growing and loving?

My mom, Frances Norris Parker, always spoke of her birth at home in Holly Springs, North Carolina. The house still stands there today. Over the years, her grandparents, Walter and Lina Banks Norris Adams, told her about the day of her delivery. In her autobiography, *Tar Heel Me*, she wrote, "It was a drab, rainy day in January, and to have the warmth necessary for the young baby, they set up a bed in the dining room, next to the kitchen where the cookstove gave off more heat." (January 30, 1926) There was no central heat back then or indoor plumbing. They would use an outhouse called a privy. After she was born, she and her parents moved to a new home on their own farm. They moved several times within the first three years of my mother's life, from Holly Springs, then to Raleigh.

My mother's dad, Walter, had been very ill with depression and a series of infections in his teeth. One day he went off hunting early in the morning with the family's dog, Jigs. When he failed to return after several hours, her mother became worried. Suddenly the dog came through the door barking and wagging his tail as if he wanted someone to follow him. One of the workmen on the farm followed him into the woods. When they found her father, they saw him lying in a clump of pines and could see what had happened. He had propped the butt of his hunting shotgun against the tree and placed the muzzle against his chest. He fired the gun by pushing the trigger with a stick and shot himself in the heart.[1]
As my mother wrote in her memoirs, she was much too young to understand the ramifications of this day. She can distinctly recall her mother standing by the doorway, resting her head on the doorframe in sorrow.

---

[1] From Frances Parker's recollections in *Tar Heel Me*.

I have in my possession a copy of a letter written by my mother's grandmother to her son, Roy, mom's uncle, who lived in Framingham, MA, explaining what happened. She laments in the letter,

Monday, April 1, 1929
My Dear Son,
Here we are amidst grief and gloom. Walter committed suicide yesterday morning at 6:10. Shot himself in the heart about ½ mile from the home. We will take remains to Holly Springs for funeral and burial this afternoon. Sister is certainly brave and holding her own marvelously. It is terrible. She will live with us. Guess we will not come back here 'til the last of this week or the 1st of next. Frances begs for her Daddie all the time. It is so pitiful. Our best love. Devotedly, Mother ~ Will write more later.

It's strange for me to look at those words because there were many times when my mom wrote me letters when I was away at college and said in closing, "Our best love, Devotedly Mom and Dad." She learned this loving language from her grandmother.

A few days later, another letter was written dated April 7, 1929, with more details about the events leading up to the suicide and the arranged funeral service. The family was distraught, thinking that somehow they had missed something that would explain why their daughter's husband had taken his life. I always imagined that this occurred during the Great Depression and had assumed that perhaps there were financial issues, but it actually happened months before the stock market crashed. I'm left to believe what I read in the letter. He suffered from severe dental problems and an infection in his gums that the best doctors in Raleigh were treating. He had still become depressed and despondent before the incident. I learned that antibiotics were not widely used to treat infections until the 1940s. So he was, I can only imagine, in chronic, debilitating, and extreme pain.

Many people from the town of Holly Springs and Raleigh attended the funeral. Neighbors brought in food for the event described in detail in the letter, saying that. Aunt Alice "put out bread and coffee and was there to serve." My mom always spoke lovingly of "Aunt Alice", the family's Black cook/housekeeper. Mother told me Aunt Alice was always a part of the family. She was married to one of the farmhands and had a young son she would bring with her when she came to work.

My mom loved to go to the washhouse, where Aunt Alice washed clothes for the family. Mother recalled spending some of her best days playing with the little children of the workers in the farm's cotton fields.

In this day of concern about racism and the divide between people, I note that her father was loved and respected by all his farmworkers, both white and Black. Her grandmother wrote in her second letter that,

Several from Manchester came, and so many of the tenants and white people from the farm came. You should have seen the number of colored people. All his workers seem to appreciate him and love him. We have never seen so many people in this town at any service. It is so sad.

What did my mother remember about those sad days? She always told me she doesn't remember being sad. She recalled tramping through the woods with her brother, Jarvis. When her short legs got tired, he would carry her on his back. She remembered sitting with her grandfather on the front porch while he churned the butter. She used to reach up and touch his scratchy beard and laughingly say, "It tickles!" Mother continued to be well-loved and cared for by her grandma and grandpa for many years.

When her mother got sick in March of 1932, the family again moved a bed into the kitchen to care for her there. She was being treated for breast cancer, and there was nothing more that doctors could do. One day after she had come home from the hospital and seemed much more cheerful and healthy, mother went to play at Cousin Betty's home across the street. Cousin Betty was a distant cousin who had no children of her own. Mom loved to go over there and bang on her organ making lots of loud "music." Later that same day, Jarvis came over to get little Franny. He told her as they walked home, "Mother's gone."

When we took our trip to North Carolina in 2006, my mother recognized Cousin Betty's house as we came back toward town. She was so full of excitement, and I could tell her mind was remembering. She looked across the street and said, "There's Cousin Betty's house!" She told me she had spent a lot of time there when her mother was ill, a time of great sadness for the entire Norris family with two young children left to be cared for, Jarvis (14) and little 6-year-old Frances.

People like Cousin Betty, who were so kind to her and loved her, helped my mother thrive.

Adoption

In the spring of 1932, after the death of her mother, Lina Banks Norris Adams, my mother Frances moved up North to Framingham, Massachusetts, with her Aunt Marguerite and Uncle Roy. Auntie Ruth and Uncle Henry drove her up to Massachusetts, stopping in the big city of New York to buy new shoes and my mom's first real ring, a gift from her Auntie Ruth. When she arrived, she suddenly had a sister, Carolyn, three years older. Mom gratefully took over Carolyn's tricycle and zoomed up and down Raymond Street![2] Her aunt and uncle were loving and strict, expecting good grades in school and excellent manners. She said, "I wasn't an 'A' student. However, I did receive honors for achievement, leadership, and service."[3] She often spoke of the day she went to court to finalize the adoption and be welcomed formally into the family.

The judge asked her, "Do you want to live here in Framingham and be part of this family?"

"Yes!" she replied with much enthusiasm. She felt happy and lucky to be there even though she missed her brother and grandparents very much.

My mom Frances learned to be gracious and well-mannered, always helped out at home, and especially loved helping her father in the garden. Fran was always happiest outside in the garden or looking out the window at the beauty of her surroundings, especially when she lived on the lake in Milton, Wisconsin. She enjoyed looking out at the treetops until the day she peacefully died in her sleep in January of 2021.

Jigs

Mom remembered Jigs, the dog, well. The black dog is pictured in several of the photographs of mom from her old photo album from Holly Springs. She had a powerful memory of Jigs coming back the

---

[2] From *Tar Heel Me*, the autobiography of Frances Norris Parker

[3] From Frances Parker's memoirs; *Grandmother Remembers.*

day her dad Walter died. She also remembered Jigs living with them until her Grandma Norris (Herselia) moved out of the old house. Mom recalled that Jigs only had three legs at that time and was a faithful pet.

The Gun [4]

When Mom and I visited North Carolina in 2006, I listened carefully as Bob, my mom's cousin, told the story about the day that Walter died by suicide and how his daddy, Robert Morrison Sr., went out to the field to retrieve the gun. He then took the gun home to get rid of it, as the Norris family did not want to keep it for obvious reasons. But they didn't get rid of it. His father kept the gun and eventually had it cleaned and used it for hunting. They would go out and hunt quail, squirrels, and rabbits. When he was a bit older, Bob's father eventually gave the gun to him, and he continued to use it for hunting. It was a quality gun, an Ithaca, and is now over 100 years old. Bob's son, Ernest Morrison, currently owns the gun. He has had the gun cleaned and has it on display in his home.

Because it is a valuable antique, and because of the story of the firearm in our family, the gun stays where it is, in Atlanta, Georgia.

Oh! If I could just have one more hour with my mother now that she's gone! I would love to write the happy ending and have the complete story instead of playing it out only in my head and imagination. I suspect that Mom has received the answers she longed for and that she has been reunited with her beloved parents now in the spiritual world. I believe that her questions have already been answered.

---

[4] Story taken from oral history shared by Bob Morrison, cousin of Frances Parker.

A Journey to the West by *Jean Roberts*

Editor's Note: The following is a work of historical fiction.

This is a copy of a letter my sister Jeanne sent to our Aunt Margareta in Detroit in 1840.

From - Jeanne Roberts, Indianapolis
To - Margareta Boots, Detroit
Written at Indianapolis, July 15, 1840

Esteemed Aunt,

With apologies for my tardiness, I write to tell of our arrival in Indianapolis and the events of our journey. My sister Katie and I left Detroit in early spring, mourning the sad loss of our parents in that terrible house fire. I am ever so grateful that you and Uncle have supported us and supported this journey with Mother's estate.

We departed Detroit by boat on May 10, and took a sideways trip north to a peculiar spit of land reaching into Lake Erie. Called Point Pelee, this is a place where vast numbers of birds gather in the Spring, and so it was that on May 12 we saw waves and clouds of winged beasts calling and landing at the water's edge. I wonder if all of Canada can be populated by these birds, there are so many.

We returned to our intended route to the destination of Toledo, arriving on May 15. Curiously, the new states of Michigan and Ohio are in dispute over who owns Toledo. Before now, no one wanted it! But since the drainage of the great swamp, both do. Nevertheless we landed at port and connected to the Erie-Wabash canal, where we boarded a packet boat and headed West toward the new state of Indiana.

The boats are drawn by mules pulling ropes alongside the canal and move about five miles per hour, stopping at nightfall. Accommodations are available at every overnight stop, either in a tavern or staying on the boat. It seems that every stop I had to evaluate which option would be safer for us two women. The canal goes west-southwest into Indiana and is being extended still farther. We stayed on the canal for most of a week, moving slowly through the landscape. There is a tremendous growth of towns and settlements along the canal. This country is changing rapidly.

At a settlement called Peru we left the canal, disembarking on its south side, and then we traveled south east, going overland by wagon to the Salamonie River, a region with peacefully settled Indians. We visited Chief Frances Godfroy's trading post called "Mount Pleasant" and saw a peaceful Indian Town. I met a family who has lived with the Miami Indians for many years. The mother was a white woman, called Maconakwa, the "Little Bear Woman" in the language of the Miami. They were concerned about rumors that their land would be seized by the many new settlers.

We stayed in this region a little while 'til we could find transport to Anderson, where there are earth mounds sacred to the Indians. There I heard a legend of the little people: "the little wild men of the forest", 24 inches tall and dressed in dark robes, who are seen darting and hiding in the woods. I did not see any of these little people myself.

The final leg of our journey, again by wagon, was south toward Indianapolis, which is building its way into the new little city. As we neared it, we came upon the National Road, the Cumberland Trail. There we drove on a temporary road alongside construction of the highway. Have you ever seen anything like this? A road beside a road. Two roads, and yet we moved slower than ever we had in the country.

As of July 10 we are lodging in a traveler's hotel on the east side of the city. Presently we are to arrange more permanent housing and hope to find a way of life. We both need new clothes after the journey, yet we arrived low on funds. I would like to teach or to assist a biological researcher. Katie would like to nanny some children. We may have to pay for room and board by doing a lady's house work, but we both have a desire to learn some higher skills, and we have been taught fine penmanship and manners. We became closer together during our journey and wish to stay together.

So we are looking ahead to the new challenges and grateful for this opportunity to build a new life. As to the people in this new land, they are pleasant, optimistic, energetic; they want to flourish like blades of grass or maybe like the great numbers of birds we saw.

Dear Aunt, wish us luck and send us your blessings. We send you the same and look forward to your next missive.

With warm regard, your nieces,
Jeanne Roberts
Katie Roberts

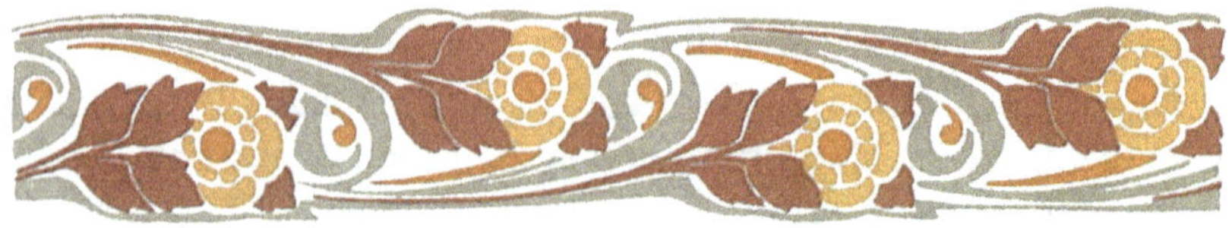

Freely *by Chuck Kellum*

Brush-stroke your nipples across my chest.
Massage my thigh in pubic pleasure.
Whisper breath upon my neck.
Soothe and tingle me all over
with fingertips and lips and
Pierce my sight with your softest gaze.

Let me roam
The terrain of your fleshly landscape,
Relishing the familiar and
Discovering the not yet known,
Ascending to throb and quiver,
And probing, probing . . .
The depths of sensitivity,
Of pleasure,
In you.

Meld with me in
Strength, power, fervor,
Tenderness, attentiveness, surrender.

In the spell of an hour, a fleeting
Flash of forever,
May we give each other
As best that best can be.

A flying visit to the villages makes one sick, cringe, reprove, and realize the ugly scars of deforestation. Insensitive cutting and burning of trees is rampant. Who doesn't know that living trees absorb and store carbon dioxide? It looks like some mean people have resolved at all costs to take us back to the Dark Ages.

When I visit urban centres, I am greeted by fumes from cars. Fumes. Furious fumes. I sometimes fume, too. Choking and shocking. *Transportation and deforestation are accomplices behind the climate change crisis*, I squeal!

When I tell people to wake up and arrest the effects of climate change, they say, *How dare you. How can you say they should not use planes, their countless and beautiful cars, and reduce livestock farming, and coal? Are you mad*, they scream and wonder. *What kind of a normal farmer would say let us reduce the use of fertilizers and livestock farming? That's utter insanity*, they say.

Do people not see the damage that looks us in the face? Floods which sweep away people, buildings, and trees. Extreme heat. Oh, sometimes it's hellish. Beasts are dying. Wildfires are causing mayhem and destruction. The weather patterns are being disobeyed and disturbed.

The planet is not happy. It needs peace and protection. Then there is the political foolery in the country. Maybe aliens are laughing at us.

My country is in a mess. Rights are a rare commodity. Some say Rights are the thighs of a tortoise. Courts. Captured. Unseen. Master Corruption rules and ruins.

I am sick to the bone about it all. The moment I meet other nationalities and we chit-chat about it, I feel lost, let down, and naked. It weighs on my pride, personality, and achievements. To be frank, this curse haunts me like a hound. Excruciating bruises are written all over me, all over my place and conscience. It is a shattered dream that haunts me day in and day out. It is so mind-boggling that it clouds the horizons of my imagination and determination.

The other day I sneaked out of my office while my immediate boss, who since morning had been either reading the foreign newspaper or phoning his friends overseas, was dozing off and frothing at the mouth. I was not sneaking out because I was on the verge of throwing up. The elders have a saying: the one (meaning the eagle) that soars about has a chance of catching (probably a chick). And so, like a roving eagle, I bumped into my former neighbour who is affectionately if not notoriously referred to as Mr. Patriot Anarchy.

He is now a salad or one of those who live in the low-density suburbs. I am still a *tshwalala* (thick maize porridge eater living in a "township"), though there is absolutely no mealie meal to cook *isitshwala* (pap/maize meal) with.

For the majority of the low-density suburbanites who have no constant supply of groceries from those in the Diaspora, even to talk of eating salads would be tantamount to lying through the teeth. Hunger rules supreme whether one is a rustic dweller or a town fellow. The farmers they chased away from the land are in neighbouring countries and overseas.

Does it make sense to kick out productive farmers, and the next thing that happens is you are seen in those "unwanted" countries where these "unwanted" people are? What are you doing there? It turns out you are actually begging for money and mercy, of course! You chased away the farmers, and then you import food produced by them from the very countries to which they fled. Who is delusional and demented here? Who has the last laugh? Please, c'mon, get real! These are precious people's lives and destinies we are discussing here. Bread and butter issues. Get a life or get a boot. The people are calling for the scalps of all bigoted bunglers.

Back to Mr. Anarchy. Upon catching sight of me, he teased: *Hunger has a way of making people fat like pigs.*

I reluctantly shook his rough and greasy hands, and responded, *Pigs eat everything. The elders say nobody knows what made pigs fat. But here there is nothing to eat, even my bones are emasculated. There is no cruelty and witchcraft worse than this!*

You know what he said upon being questioned as to why he was putting on a few kilos in the middle of a desert of basic food shortages? He smiled, revealing teeth that were not yellowish from relentless pulls of the cigarettes but rather from the foulness of his breath, epitomized as the patent effects of a long-concluded divorce between his mouth and any form of toothpaste. *I know you have slunk out of the office to join one of those endless stale bread queues! The police, as you know, respect no queue. Sometimes if you are lucky enough to get a loaf, you would have to battle with a constipation problem or a running tummy.*

I responded rather cautiously, *The police in this country promote corruption and disorder. And you may be tempted to keep your mouth shut for fear of emitting stale aroma! I think robotic police officers will do a better job. Robots don't beg for favors or bribes.*

I saw him subconsciously or intentionally muffle his mouth with his right hand. In response to my aforementioned question, words of finality he delivered with a renewed zest and zeal. *As long as queues keep on snaking and shortages persist, I prosper, for in confusion I surely prosper. I prosper under dubious and opaque circumstances. I thrive well under the shadow of darkness. I used to have meetings with the sons and daughters of Mr. Inflation, but now during the day or night I mingle and mix with Mr. Inflation Senior. I mean Sir Hyper-inflation!*

That is Mr. Anarchy for you. The man who decided to lose his soul and senses in pursuit of a life of spreading lies and confusion in the name of keeping the ruining party's leader and his shenanigans, doing what they know best, ruining first and mis-ruling forever and ever amen.

He is the same lousy praise singer I told in the face a few months ago to go hang on Mount Party Marionettes and fall headlong with all the king's acolytes ready to sing songs of heroic patriotism (instead of blatant partisanship), after he declared his sexual lust for me. He actually whispered to me sensually, *Night is right for this. I will be your moon to give you a series of unforgettable moans.*

I was not going be a sex object for him or any other man in this man-made hell. I told him to go to hell and burn in eternity. My words stung him into silence. In fact, he looked like a hot-water doused cock! His colleagues preach powerful and sorrowful messages about the importance of fidelity in the face of the AIDS pandemic year in year out, yet most of them are busy buying concubines and mistresses with money meant for poor AIDS patients.

They have contributed significantly, and couldn't care less, to the total collapse of the health system. There is rapid deterioration of the health service delivery system, lack of adequate water supply, and lack of capacity to dispose of solid waste and repair sewage blockages, which all contribute to the escalation and spread of many contagious diseases.

The selfish leaders are not worried to death. Why? Because they are out of touch with the rest of the citizens, and can fly out of the kingdom at the slightest scream of their bulging stomachs, or when their imported groceries run out. They zip from galaxy to galaxy, time to time. Their universe is painted with lots and lots of sunshine and fun, yet they keep pushing ours toward a certain dystopia.

The dream. All shattered. The brave sons and daughters of the struggle paid the supreme price, deep in their hearts and heads were treasures of regaining dignity, land, and their rights as citizens. Their songs were loud and clear, harping on freedom of association, press freedom, and other tenets of democracy. The blood-thirsty emperor has made a mockery of Prince Franchise.

This is a very sad state of affairs, because all the sons and daughters of Mr. Scam and Mrs. Sham (or is it Shame?) take center stage whenever ballot time comes. These sons and daughters team up with such dirty-minded people like Mr. Anarchy and run roughshod over Prince Franchise.

I am bleeding in my heart as I report that Sir Democracy has gone AWOL. I heard him with my ears. *I shall only return when there is sanity.*

Those were his words before he escaped. There is a humanitarian, political, social, and economic catastrophe that should galvanize the decent souls to put their heads together and seek a lasting solution.

But … I do not know. Economic meltdown is taking its toll. Political rape is suffocating and submerging all the voices of reason and dissent. It is a disgrace. I mean a calamity plus a bottomless pity. I am outraged. Were our gigantic dreams of freedom, navigation, and advances in science and technology just a piece of utopia?

Friend, this is an open secret. The emperor and Sir Democracy are like oil and water. You know what, Sir Democracy was on the minefield the very moment he declared no person had a right to foist hunger, penury, and dehumanization on the poor in the name of promoting and protecting autocracy for eternity. Sir Democracy, being frank and open as he is, thoroughly rapped the emperor and the royal cronies for dining and wining without a care on the innocent blood of our fallen heroes and heroines. He also slammed His Majesty for brutalizing Prince Franchise and all the people who supported the prince. The bootlickers did not mince their words, they said he was treading where angels fear. Call to mind, those people have made it their duty to feel pain for him, and if it were possible, they would cough and cringe for him!

I look up to Sir Democracy. I doff my hat to Prince Franchise. Both epitomize our struggle for dignity, freedom, and normalcy. I also salute Miss Equality.

One dark night, the so-called Owls visited her. She was battered and insulted for exercising her constitutional right to express her views and opinions. Miss Equality, diminutive heroine, was fast asleep, dreaming about time travel, teleportation, telepathy, mind control, telekinesis, space travel and exploration, mutants, aliens, extraterrestrial lifeforms, interplanetary warfare, parallel universes, and fictional worlds when one royal member attempted to rape her. For all his troubles, she kicked his testicles nice and fast, Will Smith-style, until he passed out! Actually, the dazed culprit put his fingers between his legs, as if to prove whether the "kitchen utensils" were still there or there was no more ball to be played!

Later, as assertive as ever, she told people attending a residents meeting that only idiotic women went into paroxysms of jubilation and praise singing after being given a mere piece of meat before an election.

Hunger stalks the land for the majority, but a certain dish of fish called propaganda does not run out. Hardly a day passes by without one watching those gigantic fish on TV. These vertebrate cold-blooded animals with grills are portrayed by the overzealous bootlickers as real and nutritious.

Miss Equality was arrested for writing in the local paper that what people were actually hearing was nothing but verbal diarrhea. She was castigated for saying there is a lot of hand-clapping, handshaking, pontificating, or posturing, whilst the kingdom was going up in flames. I was moved by her words that day. *Brothers and sisters, speak out. Tell the world your story. Don't wait for a Moses to descend from heaven. Tell yourself you are your own Moses. Did not our wise elders say: the Rock Rabbit has no tail because of his dependence on the generosity of others? Similarly, didn't our seniors warn us about a thing that belongs to someone else? They did. They said a thing that belongs to someone else is the gravy of the hyena.*

Upon meeting her in the food queues people ululated, chanting, *Our Lady Moses*. True! A plough that belongs to someone else cannot be banked on for a good harvest. If a tyre has a puncture, what do we do? You would say: *mend the tyre*. If a soccer coach is giving fans no joy but a series of failures and excuses, what do we do? Yes, we show the bungler the red card! The exit!

Did I mention that Miss Equality escaped from the police station? Not before she smashed the handcuffs into smithereens! One police officer's body shivered and welled up with a great grandparent of terror and begged for her mercy. Master Corruption is the official way of conducting business here, and he called Miss Equality names, including *poisonous witch*, *genetically superior smug subhuman*, and *uncultured, westernized street-girl*. Master Corruption actually leapt in the air like one possessed, hit his chest five times, and declared no Western-indoctrinated woman should talk as if she has what men have between their legs! Master Corruption was furious that Miss Equality had managed to free all the women who had been bundled into the back of a truck and detained in a prison, whose toilets were flushed once per week, for two months, eating maize porridge once a day.

As a woman, I look at the innocent children whose future has been ruined and tears start to cascade down my cheeks. There has to be a better life. Is this a life, really? Do we deserve all these debasing experiences? What about the children whose future has been turned into doom and gloom? What sin have they committed? Their schools are nothing but some white elephant. There is no schooling to talk of, unless one can afford to pay a private tutor in foreign currency for extra lessons. The hospitals and clinics are devoid of any form of medication under the sun. No pill. No nothing.

Absolutely horrifying institutions. No longer life-saving centres. Not anymore. People just pray that they do not fall sick. How precarious a life this is. And cholera is always lurking. It is and was always coming … no wonder, for where are the chemicals to treat the water? Innocent people are dying like flies. Yet there is always money for rallies to demonise the opposition, the West, and for flying overseas to pontificate about our independence and successes as a people! And the world listens … or does it?

There are the senseless killings and a wave of violence, fear, indoctrination, discrimination, and intimidation. Who shall put out this inferno of madness? Are the players not putting their selfish and personal agenda ahead of the plight of the majority? My hope will not perish in this suffering and the collapsing of the kingdom. Somebody else? No. I am a woman of strength, endurance and with a vision. Just as the fallen heroes and heroines had a dream, I also need to dream anew. Most of my countrymen are scattered all over the world. It is also true that there is no currency in this kingdom, only something people call "burial cheques" (meaning money has been laid to rest in the cemetery of corruption). To make matters worse, banks time and again run out of those useless but numerous papers.

I personally shall not whimper, but do something about this decay, this conflagration, this stench, and this imprisonment. My homeland has turned into a Kingdom of Muddle, Misery, and Madness, but I have a burning desire to transform it into a Heaven of Hope, Prosperity, and Unity. Rebuilding and healing starts with me. National radio and TV stations are powerful media houses, rooted on one side of the coin. Is it possible that all the people who are interviewed there think alike?
No, the question should be: *what can or should I do?* I will tell my story with vigour irrespective of all the indignities l have suffered. An African proverb spells it out: *until the lions get their own historian the tale of the hunt will always glorify the hunter*.

I will work with people who love our county, our continent, and our planet. I see a number of villagers planting trees and reducing livestock farming. In urban centres, I see people getting involved in local and political advocacy on issues of climate change. They have made personal choices in such areas as diet, household energy use, long-and-short distance travel, consumption of goods and services, and family size. Kids are showing greater interest in conservation and minimalism.

There is a ray of hope at the end of the tunnel. Miss Equality is our heroine. She says she will import advanced technology, knowledge, and powers from other places and planets. We know she is capable because she can travel to other spaces and at different paces with ease and charm. She flies and conquers for us. Our victorious heroine.

Because Of Leaves *by Alys Caviness-Gober*

Watching the leaves let go
either in a downward drifting slow
descent as if embraced by loving arms
eager to cushion the fall,
or when the letting go is
a crashing into earth, a rough blow-down
by November's bristling breath,
now
in this softened morning light,
when their colors glow with faded warmth,
then because of leaves,
missing you hurts
even more.

Autumn Leaves *by Alys Caviness-Gober*

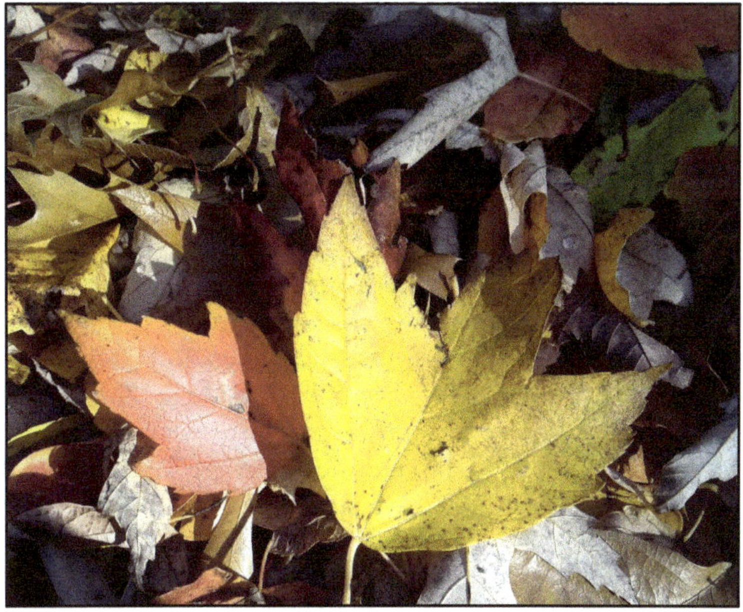

Samhain[5] *by Mairéad Lewis* 

comes *aos sí*[6] this night
through the *féth fiadha*[7] thin
daoine maithe[8] hither now —
look up and see *cailleacha*[9]
flit across the yellow moon

---

[5] *Samhain* (s**aw**-when): Gaelic; a Gaelic festival marking the end of the harvest season and beginning of winter or "darker-half" of the year; in 2021 *Samhain* is on Sunday, 31 October 31.

[6] *aos sí* (ees-sh**ee**): older form Irish/Gaelic; Tuath Dé (tribe of the gods) or Tuatha Dé Danann (People of the goddess Danu), the ancient Irish race of gods, founded by the goddess Danu; a supernatural race in Irish mythology.

[7] *féth fiadha* or *féth Fíadha* (feth f**ee**-uhta): Gaelic; magic mist (of the Knower), veil between living humans and the Otherworld.

[8] *daoine maithe* (dw**ee**nuh-m**a**ha): Irish/Gaelic; the good people (the dead; spirits; faeries).

[9] *cailleacha* (k**ey**ll-uhch-uh): Irish/Gaelic; witches; plural of *cailleach* (witch).

The Witching Hour *by David Allen*

Last night I was awake
at the Witching Hour, staring
at a blank computer screen.
It was 3AM, but I wasn't tired,
believing, perhaps, the full moon
and silent night would conspire
to aid me in finding the words
for a new poetic masterpiece.
But my inner critic laughed,
rejecting lines and rhymes.
Alliterations were flung aside,
axed, and archived.
The minutes ticked by
until a whistle blew
announcing coffee brewed
in the kitchen.

Golden Field 2 *by Sarah E. Morin*

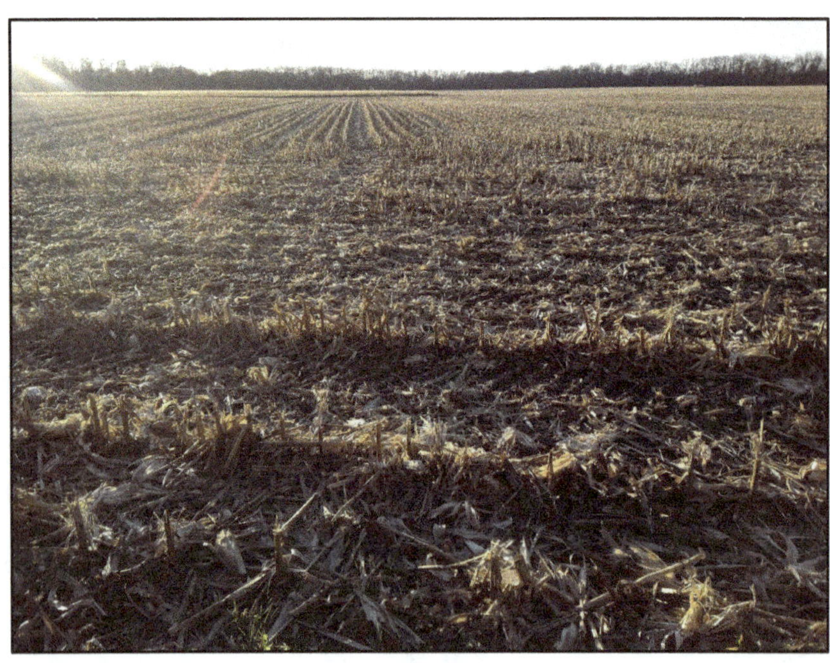

***Untitled** by JAC, B. Monét, Z. Rose*

Take time for thyself
I command you to stop
wish upon a star, for old times' sake
remember a time we went by the lake
you would tell me stories

The weight of your voice carries for hours
Didn't you know you live in the pit of my mind
the silence at night I welcome as comfort
but come morning and the souls of my feet stand to fight
walking around aimlessly, I listen to your voice
dreaming of a fantasy, wishing upon a reality
a reality where a gift of an hour can ease the anxiety shriveling inside of me

Silent at times, but today pressing my temples
I live for the feeling of love, but I'm floating
no other way of life, but others live through
fighting freedom, frequent fliers fire fools
wanting more but unable to reach my temple

Happiness turned upside down
Wanting a parallel universe to become home

the world spun once from your tremendous gravity
toiling away to just keep you amused and burning bright
all due to an explosion long ago, brilliant beyond all velocity
becoming desolate and polluted with each revolution around
bathed in the shine of another sun's embrace
long gone yet still reaching, searing the empty abyss
pulls apart what once came together, in a golden hour

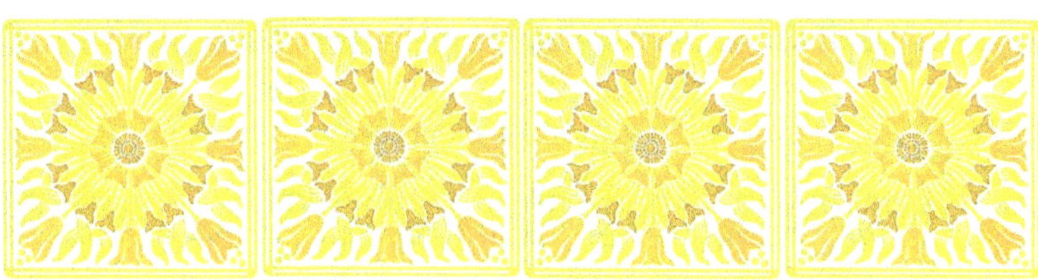

1980s Filmstrip Day *by Jenny Kalahar* 

I'm speaking to those who remember that a film
can suddenly melt,
white light replacing images,
that the immersion into another world can be broken –
a projector overheats,
a snag in a strip causes a break,
and a reel of film goes *flap-flap-flap*
until solid whiteness comes.
And I'm speaking to those
who then suddenly remember
that they're in a classroom
filled with slightly sweaty teenagers,
tired after gym class,
who were drifting off into memories,
or wishes, or fantasies,
or actually watching
a hippo mother guiding her baby
across a muddy pond
in a lush country they may never see.
Startled, they remember
the hardening, pink wad of gum in their mouth
and start chewing again.
Notice their laces are untied.
Remember with trepidation that algebra is next,
and a test they didn't really study for,
and they have to pick up a little brother or sister
from elementary school
and take care of them
until unhappy parents get home.

I'm speaking now to the screen gone blank
after the geography teacher switches on the room lights.
You'll never know what comes next in the film.
You're snapped into your roller
and held breathless
until a week from Thursday
when World War II comes to room sixteen.
You've seen that one before.

You've seen the marching lines of soldiers passing Hitler,
faces turned to the monster.
You've seen the trenches,
and how young the boys just their age
were turned into lost old men inside.
You've seen the bombs bursting on buildings,
and those now-familiar ladies and children
running for their lives.
You'll relive it all a week from Thursday,
and for twenty years to come.

Face-to-face With A Faceless Face *by Ndaba Sibanda* 

the sun had rolled and retired
into the cheerful cuddle of its mom,
giving way to a dense dusk to dance,
and nocturnal creatures to creep,
shamble and sing their silly songs,
later, she was stomping and singing
in a bid to give herself a false sense
of fearlessness, freeness, and fun,
a hunch herded her to turn around
and take an abrupt look, and Lord!
there was something unfamiliar
about the fast fellow's familiarity,
she couldn't figure out who he was,
but his gaiety appeared like a sight
his eyes were used to slapping on,

but who is he? what is he up to?
is he rushing to catch up with me?
would he not harm me? would he say
hi? would he propose to me? would
he accept a direct or diplomatic snub?

there was an air of awkwardness,
quickness and foreignness about him
that made her hair to stand on end:
who is this long-limbed loose rover?
look at his robotic speed, his lankiness!

if only I had a cheetah's legs that are longer
and leaner than those of other cats . . . then
I would lift them off the ground and cross them
underneath my body while bounding along!
If a were a horse I would lengthen my stride
and transition from a careful, cute canter
to a faraway flying and fierce gallop,
if a hole could just heave up and swallow
me up, if I had left home earlier . . . if . . .
if that man had just left me alone . . .

she lamented, labored, reflected;
pondered, prayed as she purred;
was he an alien with a faceless face?
the shadowy lanky loner paced
past her quaking frame without
as much as a care or a sound
along a fine forested footpath,
as a result a mammoth mass
of gathered firewood fell off
her flighty flummoxed head!

Golden Hour on the White River *by Sarah E. Morin*

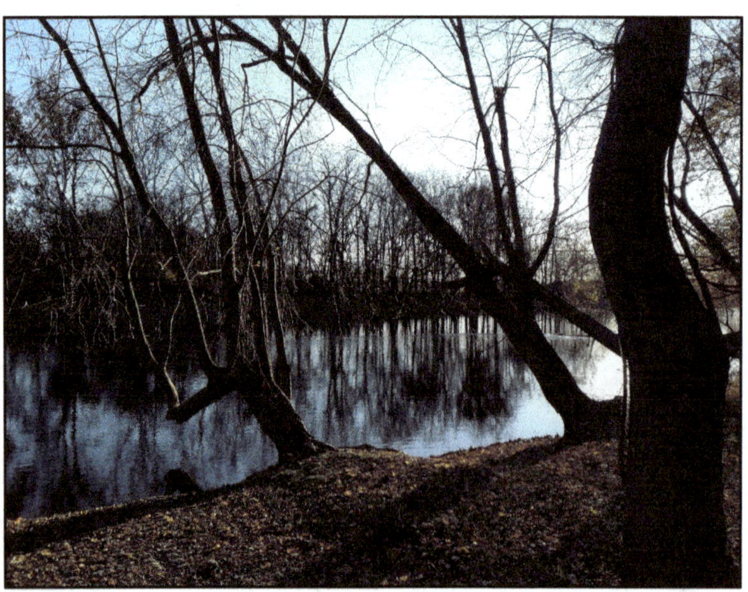

Cockatiel on a Flowered Branch *by Jerry Dreesen*

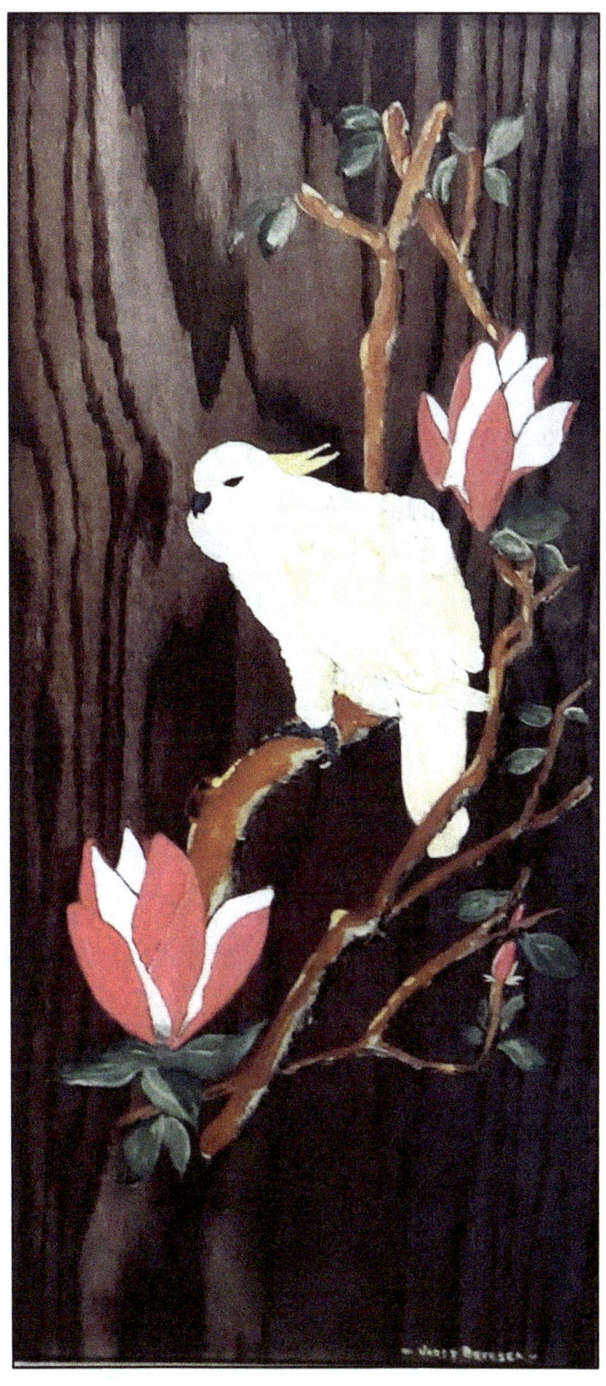

His Gift Of Time *by Marilyn J Wolf*

Many years ago
I was dating a man
who:
worked full-time
traveled for work
was studying for his MBA
was a part-time father, and
tried to have a minimal social life.
During dinner at his house,
which he had prepared,
I was whining that
I didn't get to spend enough time with him.
He put down his silverware
stared at his plate for a few seconds
and turned to me.

He said,
"I give you the most precious thing I have.
My time."

I never mentioned it again.

Pond Flowers *by Alys Caviness-Gober*

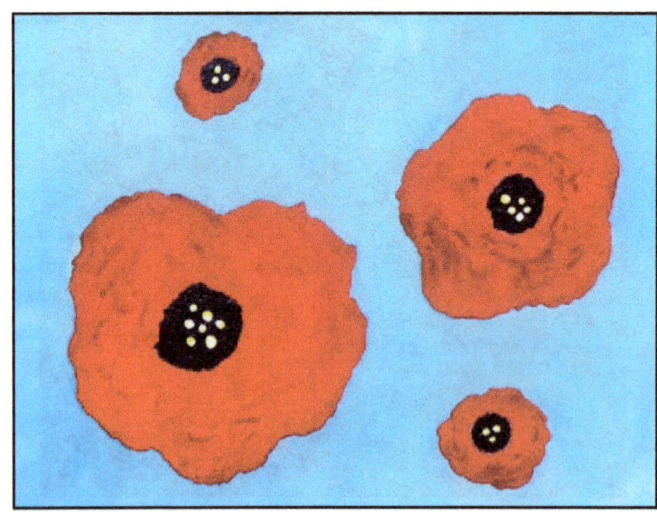

One By One *by Chuck Kellum*

One

By

One

They pass

Away.

First the

Times,

Then the

People

With the

Memories,

And then

Finally

Even the

Ones

Who

Remember them.

My Secret Camera *by Patrick Kalahar* 

This is the Age of Narcissism,
the culture of self-congratulation.
Nothing exists till it has been duly labeled
and quantified in relation to ourselves.
The dominant form of expression of our time is the selfie
Here is ME (Taj Mahal in the background)
Here is ME (Temple of the Olympian Zeus in the background)
Here is ME (Grand Canyon in the background)
There are museums where the exhibits are set up for selfies.
The whole world exists only as backdrop for ourselves,
monuments to our own self-importance.

But I, too, take pictures with my secret camera,
the lenses are my eyes
and the plates are burned in silver and platinum
on the cells of my brain.
My secret camera photographs
the forgotten, the outcast, the eccentric,
the weird and the wonderful, people with a whole lifetime,
a culture, a cosmography etched on each face.
My secret camera also photographs
the great monuments of nature and of man
without people and, emphatically, without myself.
My secret camera photographed the Coliseum as magnificent ruin,
and at the same time complete and filled with ghosts of a thousand years.
My secret camera also photographed the Temple of the Olympian Zeus,
its pillars impossibly high,
stark and majestic,
supporting the weight of a Greek sky
so impossibly blue
that to capture it exactly
would grant one a place among the gods.

Our secret cameras
take the only photographs
worth preserving.

Time Is Irrelevant *by Alys Caviness-Gober*

Days and nights have neither minutes nor hours,
and there is no ticking away,
no sand falling, no silent digital flip.

Time is irrelevant
where Grief lives.

Grief invites Memories
to come unbidden,
erasing Time,
obscuring Time,
ending Time.

Memories contain your aery laughter,
carried by salty pacific seaside breezes and
midwestern humidity and icy winds,
and Memories contain the ethereal butterfly wings
of your voice, a lilt that cannot be imitated;
it was yours alone,
and it was mine whenever you
said my name out loud.

Time is irrelevant
where Grief lives,
but Grief invites Memories,
and Memories contain you,
so I have no need of Time.
I live where Grief lives, and
I'm content.

About *Polk Street* and *The Polk Street Review* anthology

The Polk Street Review book is named in honor of a significant historic Noblesville street originally named after William Conner's partner, Josiah Polk. It is now called 8th Street. The street dates to 1823 when Noblesville was laid out; it is the north/south road that used to have railroad tracks running alongside and down the middle of it (the historic Heritage Railway tracks were removed by the City of Noblesville a few years ago, and trains that ran through Noblesville for almost 200 years are gone forever). Mills were at the north end of the street, and the old courthouse, bars, liveries, hotels, homes, and other buildings of industry lined its southern stretch.

At some point in Noblesville's history, Polk Street became the dividing line between white-collar and blue-collar neighborhoods, white and black neighborhoods, residential and industrial areas, and high ground *versus* the flood plain. Over time those divisions became so ingrained that people didn't mention them, but they "knew" them. Social and economic division are like that: they take on a life of their own unless we consciously resist them, because they become taken for granted, like history itself.

A lot of folks today see 8th Street as just a main route through town, but the old road represents the true history of Noblesville, her businesses, and the generations of people who have lived here. Noblesville continues to see a lot of change as developers have their way, but we believe it can retain its unique historic small-town qualities while recognizing that certain areas, certain landmarks, and certain streets are playing a part in the City's vision for the future. In today's developer-driven world, we hope that Noblesville can remain a special place with a small-town feel.

Our annual anthology project, *The Polk Street Review*, celebrates the heritage, history, and people connected to Noblesville ~ past and present ~ in submissions of original prose, poetry, song lyrics, and artwork images. In the past, we asked that either the subject matter or the submitter have a connection to Noblesville, but as our organization has grown a global audience we've opened submissions to a diverse global arts community.

You may wonder about the grasshopper in the original TPSR logo:

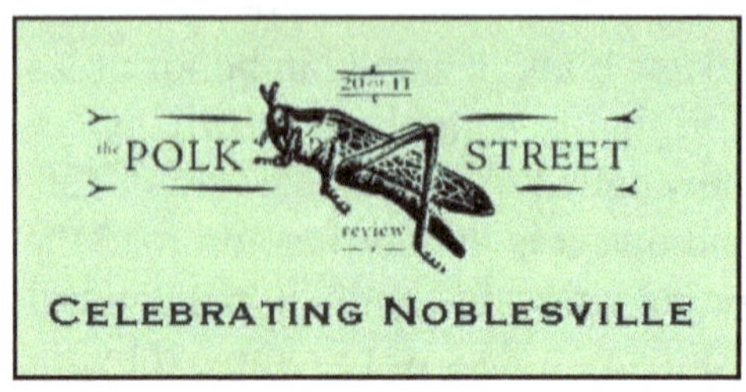

We often refer to our contributors as *grasshoppers* and to the people who quietly support them as *ants.* These insect references are taken from Aesop's fable, *The Ant & The Grasshopper*. Grasshoppers are the dreamers, the creatives: we artists, writers, and musicians. Ants are support us: our hardworking loved ones toiling away in the background. Grasshoppers create that which feeds the soul; ants create that which feeds the body. The world needs both ants and grasshoppers, so cheers to both!

About *Community • Education • Arts, Inc.* (CEArts)

Community • Education • Arts, Inc. (CEArts) is a 501(c)(3) nonprofit Arts organization that is based in Noblesville with a global reach. Our organization is run by three dedicated people volunteering their time so that CEArts can continue to host online *Arts Showcase* exhibits on our website, record @theroundtable arts podcast, and our two annual projects: our classic literature-based project, *Noblesville Interdisciplinary Creativity Expo* (NICE), and *The Polk Street Review* project. A special *thank you* to our Volunteer Board Officers:

President: Alys Caviness-Gober *Secretary*: Sarah E. Morin
Treasurer: Joyce Perry

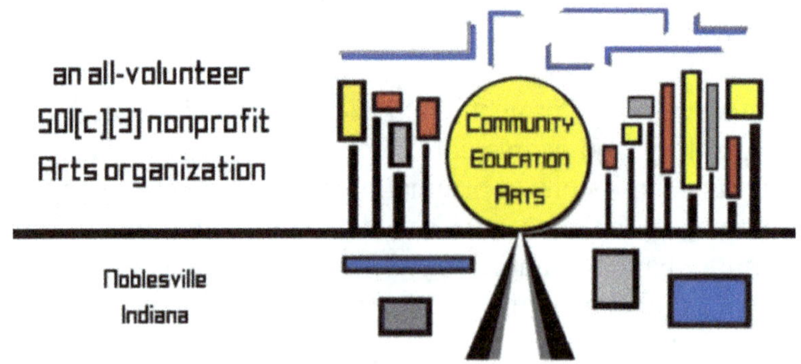

David Allen is a retired journalist who worked on newspapers in New York, Virginia, Indiana, and the Far East. He is a former vice president and contest director for the Poetry Society of Indiana. Allen has four books of poetry for sale on Amazon. Visit his blog at www.davidallen.nu.

Kathy Bell & Bob McGilpin
Kathy Bell (Ma Bell) began at an early age with a dream to perform and sing at the Grand Ole Opry. At 10 years of age, she was playing the piano and singing at the church where her grandfather pastored. In high-school, Kathy played flute in band and sang alto with the choir. Shortly after, she began writing songs and going to Nashville, TN to the songwriter festival. Kathy competed in costume in Karaoke competitions and did well, leading her a career as a Karaoke Host, Wedding DJ, and a fun loving, clean, comedy act called "Ma Bell". Kathy loves her music and entertainment career, and her dream is to still to perform at the Grand Ole Opry. For now, she loves sharing her music and comedy with others.
Bob McGilpin's first release was 1978's *Superstar* on Butterfly Records, which became a Billboard hit along with *Sexy Thing* and *When You Feel Love*. He had multiple major label record deals with Casablanca, RCA, and Butterfly/MCA. Competing with luminaries such as KC and The Sunshine Band and The Bee Gees, McGilpin proved his sound was equally emblematic of the era by landing three #1 hits on the coveted Billboard Dance Charts. Bob is currently working as a Producer, Songwriter, Engineer, and Designer/Builder of MVAmps.

Vivianne Belle lives in Noblesville. She enjoys traveling abroad and occasionally putting pen to paper to write poetry and prose.

John A. Caviness grew up in Noblesville, graduating from Noblesville High School, and received a Bachelor of Arts in Foreign Languages (German Studies) and Master of Science from the *Center for Communication and Information Sciences* (CICS) at Ball State University. When writing with friends Z. Rose and B. Monét, he contributes as **JAC**. John loves to fix problems, ease frustration, and optimize quality of life while working with technology. He helps the company he works for, and their clients, thrive in the modern technological landscape. John is creative and occasionally known to enjoy some odd songs and shows with a Mead in hand. He has been a male ally to women and other disenfranchised groups throughout his life and hopes he can help all people work together better in the technology space.

Alys Caviness-Gober is a disabled anthropologist, artist, and writer. She taught Anthropology, Women's Studies, and ESOL at the university level, and was a PhD candidate in Applied Linguistics until her disabilities worsened in 2009. In 2011, Alys began selling artwork (*Creative Expressions Arts*), and soon after was juried into the *Hamilton County Artists' Association* in both photography and 2D categories. Alys and author Sarah E. Morin are the cofounders of the literature-based annual project *Noblesville Interdisciplinary Creativity Expo* (NICE). In November 2014, Alys founded *Logan Street Sanctuary, Inc.* (LSS), an all-volunteer 501(c)(3) Arts organization and the organization took over hosting the annual *Noblesville Interdisciplinary Creativity Expo* (NICE) project and the publication of the annual anthology *The Polk Street Review*. In July 2019, LSS rebranded as *Community • Education • Arts* (CEArts). She is a FY2017 (July 2016 - June 2017) Indiana Arts Commission *Individual Artist Project* Grant Award recipient, for which she created a series of large-scale paintings expressing life with hidden disabilities. Alys was selected to participate in the IUPUI Arts and Humanities Institute's *Religion Spirituality, and the Arts* 2018/19 Seminar Class, and has been an invited presenter at *Poetry Society of Indiana* conferences since 2017. She is a selected poet for *INverse: Indiana's Poetry Archive*, and a member of both *Noble Poets* and the *Poetry Society of Indiana*. Alys' poetry has been featured in global anthologies since the 1980s, in the *Last Stanza Poetry Journal*, *The Polk Street Review*, and in her own poetry and artwork collections, *Naked In Wonderland (Volumes I, II, III, IV)*. She serves on the Noblesville Cultural Arts Council and is active in the local arts scene. Alys' artwork, photographs, and poetry have received national and international recognition.

Jerry Dreesen is an artist and poet, self-taught in both disciplines. He loves to challenge himself in a variety of art styles and mediums, including watercolor, acrylics, pastels, and also experiments in clay modeling and found sculptures. Jerry is a member of Nickel Plate Arts and the online gallery, Plogix. He has exhibited his work in a number of art and business venues. Jerry has sold his art throughout the US, Great Britain, Europe, and Japan.

Natalie Gaytan, pen name **B. Monét**, was born in California and raised in Indiana. She began her journey in art and poetry while in college and progressed throughout the years. Natalie's inspiration in poetry bloomed through the work of Rupi Kaur along with the inspiration to express her art from her best friend Z. Rose. With both skills combined, today she takes time to journal, express, and live a vibrant life. With the encouragement of her friends and family, and with biweekly writing sessions and art collaborations, Natalie continues to create new content and to grow through her art and words.

Jenny Kalahar is the editor and publisher of *Last Stanza Poetry Journal*. She is the author of fourteen books. Twice nominated for a Pushcart Prize and once for Best of the Web, her poems have been published in journals, anthologies, and newspapers. Her works can also be found on poemhunter.com and INverse, Indiana's poetry archive. Through her Stackfreed Press, she has published books for numerous authors.

Patrick Kalahar is a used and rare bookseller with his wife, Jenny, and a book conservationist. He is a veteran, world traveler, avid reader, and book collector. His poems have been published in several journals and anthologies. Patrick can be seen as an interviewee in the Emmy-winning documentary *James Whitcomb Riley: Hoosier Poet*, and he gives costumed and scholarly readings as Edgar Allan Poe.

Chuck Kellum grew up on a farm southwest of Indianapolis. As a young adult he traveled the world a bit – about twenty countries in all. He eventually settled into a technology-related career primarily as a business applications software developer, got and stayed married, helped raise three children, and has lived in Anderson, Indiana, since 1984. Chuck began writing poetry while a senior in college studying engineering. He wrote about 120 poems in the course of a dozen years before getting married, but then was too busy after that with work and family. Chuck resumed writing poems on a somewhat frequent basis in 2009 after he retired. He's been a member of the Noble Poets club since 2017, and currently serves as Treasurer and Contest Director of the Poetry Society of Indiana.

Dr. Leah Leach is the founder of Gal's Guide to the Galaxy, which is home to the first lending library dedicated to women's history in the United States. Before founding Gal's Guide in 2016, she ran a successful film company for a decade, winning 12 cinematic awards along the way. Leah has won six awards for the podcasts she has produced, and you can hear her weekly on the *Gal's Guide Podcast* talking about cool women of history. Dr. Leach holds an honorary degree in Metaphysics from the Universal Life Church. She has studied Joseph Campbell, Carl Jung, and Sigmond Freud. She made a solid attempt to study Nietzche but stopped because it nearly broke her positive spirit. Leah is a writer and mixed media artist. Her most recent writing work won her 3rd place in *The Polk Street Review 2020*, and her art has been on display at Nickel Plate Arts, Hub & Spoke, and Meyer Najem. Check out all things fun with Leah at her website http://leah-leach.com.

Mairéad Lewis (pr. *mih-rayd loo-whis*) is a Celtic writer and artist living in Dublin, Ireland.

Mona Mehas (she/her) writes about growing up poor, accumulating grief, and the urgency of climate change. As a retired Indiana public school teacher, she spends most days at her laptop with two old cats as chaperones. Connect with Mona at linktr.ee/ppyoung.

Gail Mehlan lives in the area with her husband, Doug. She moved here about seven years ago from the Chicago area to be close to grandchildren in Noblesville. Gail is a retired bilingual teacher. She enjoys writing and is currently working on a memoir, hoping to self-publish in 2022. Gail also loves to travel to Spain and Portugal and is looking forward to more travel experiences in the future.

Sarah E. Morin serves as a kidwrangler at Conner Prairie, a history museum in Fishers, Indiana. She has published two books, *Waking Beauty* (a Christian fantasy novel based on *Sleeping Beauty*) and *Rapunzel the Hairbrained*, a children's picture book that forms the basis of a workshop to build girls' self-esteem. Sarah E. is the Premier Poet of Poetry Society of Indiana, Secretary of *Community Education Arts*, and co-founder of *Noblesville Interdisciplinary Creativity Expo* (NICE). She loved the years she spent living above the Clock Shop in Noblesville, and still remains engaged in the downtown scene through Noble Poets (new poets welcome – 3rd Tuesday each month at 6:30pm in Zoom during the pandemic). When she grows up, she wants to be a child prodigy. Visit her at sarahemorin.com.

Mike Nierste's poetry has appeared in *Flying Island*, *Tipton Poetry Journal*, *frogpond*, and in the anthologies *Cowboys & Cocktails*, *Poetry* *from the True Grit Saloon*, *Reflections on Little Eagle Creek*, and, with this publication, *The Polk Street Review*. Mike is the author of a book of contradictory quotes and contranyms, titled *Contra-Diction*, and has self-published two poetry chapbooks, *Savor* and *Discoveries*.

Kitty O'Doherty lives in Noblesville, where she spends time with her three grandchildren, partner, and four rescue cats. She never achieved her first childhood dream of being a circus acrobat but did spend several years as a crew member for a sports car racing team – after turning 50. She would love to be a bird for a year, to float on the thermals above the earth just to enjoy the perspective. These days she enjoys writing stories from her life and walking along the river near her home, finding breathing room and inspiration in nature.

Deborah Petersen is an educator, having taught middle and high school students and a colleges level Composition professor. She has served as the President of the *Poetry Society of Indiana*, as well as a Poetry Contest judge for national and state contests. Deborah edited and contributed to three poetry anthologies and was a featured poet in the *Indiana Voice Journal*. Deborah that she is the living epitome of "a Word Junkie" and her first poetic influences were the prayers of her childhood. Later, she was influenced by the complexity and cadence of William Shakespeare's works, and in recent years she's been moved by the writings of Persian Poet and Sufi Mystic, Rumi, and by the Japanese *haiku* Master, Basho. As artists, Deborah believes we are mere conduits. When she is in the moment of being a conduit, she finds herself in an omniscience, a moment of vastness and grace, a connection to a universal wisdom and discerning perception.

Jean Roberts is a retired plant scientist who lives in the country in northern Hamilton County, where she grows wonderful flowers. She is also a guitar player and band leader. Jean volunteers at the Pioneer Village at the Indiana State Fair.

Z. Rose is the pen name of **Payge Gillig**, who started using the pen name when she began writing after college. Raised in Indiana with many opportunities, she found her true passion is artwork and poetry. You can find her with people working on this craft or collaborating on a project. She loves connecting with people and to the artwork at hand. This year her goal is to bring poetry into galleries, pairing poetry with diverse artworks. She loves writing and inspiring others and hopes to have her first book come out in 2022.

Ndaba Sibanda is a Bulawayo-born poet, novelist, and nonfiction writer; author of 28 published books of various genres and coauthor more than 100 published books. Ndaba's works can be found or are forthcoming in *Page & Spine, Piker Press, SCARLET LEAF REVIEW, Universidad Complutense de Madrid, the Pangolin Review, Kalahari Review, Botsotso, The Ofi Press Magazine, Hawaii Pacific Review, Deltona Howl, The song is, JONAH magazine, Saraba Magazine, Poetry Potion, Saraba Magazine, The Borfski Press, East Coast Literary Review, Whispering Prairie Press*, and *The Polk Street Review*. Sibanda has received the following nominations: the National Arts Merit Awards (NAMA), the Mary Ballard Poetry Chapbook Prize, the Best of the Net Prose, and the Pushcart Prize.
https://www.pagespineficshowcase.com/ndaba-sibanda.html
https://ndabasibanda.wordpress.com/2017/03/26/first-blog-post/
https://www.amazon.com/Books-Ndaba-Sibanda/

Nancy Simmonds is a poet from Fort Wayne, Indiana. "Connect" was Nancy's word to define her Resolution for 2021. It was a success on many levels. If you see her, she would love to hear what your word is for 2022. And why. And how. And whether or not you would let her borrow it for her next poem.

Kristine Staley is a Noblesville High School graduate. She holds degrees in Communications, Business and Public Health (Epidemiology). Kristine returned to Noblesville in 2014, started painting after attending a wine and canvas event, and now spends her time painting in oil, acrylic, and watercolor. She is very fond of her Siamese cat Mario and can frequently be seen chasing him around the yard. Kristine dreams of new opportunities in publishing her art illustrations and can be reached at Kristine.Staley9328@gmail.com.

Dr. Paul "Spike" Wilson is a poet, playwright, stage director, and theatre scholar. He is the Artistic Director of Page & Stage Co. (a theatre-for-literacy organization) and co-founder of the True Names Initiative for Drama Therapy and Social Action. His other works include a cycle of Christian-Zen poems and an anthology of literacy plays called *The Peanut Gallery*. Visit him at pageandstageco.org.

Marilyn J Wolf is a poet, author, wanderer, and is always curious. *In Celebration of the Death of Faeries* is her first book; she is currently editing a second. https://medium.com/@Wolfen25.

George Wolfe is Professor Emeritus and former Director of the Ball State University Center for Peace and Conflict Studies. He is an award-winning poet and the author of over 50 articles on the website Voices of Humanity and three books, including his latest collection of poetry entitled, *Clapping with One Hand: Poems Inspired by Zen, Mozart and my Experience of India*. His first book, *The Spiritual Power of Nonviolence: Interfaith Understanding for a Future without War*, has been endorsed by Arun Gandhi and by Judy O'Bannon, the former First Lady of Indiana. Wolfe is also an accomplished classical saxophonist who has appeared as a soloist with such ensembles as the Royal Band of the Belgian Air Force, the Saskatoon Symphony, the Chautauqua Motel Choir, and the Indianapolis Symphony Band.

2022 *The Polk Street Review* Awards

Award of Merit (*Best in Book*):
The *Award of Merit*, this year goes to George W. Wolfe for his poem, ***Verses Re-Versus no. 13***. The poem is a palindrome, in which the second stanza is the first stanza with the words written in reverse order. It is a difficult form, and George's poem is an excellent example. We also love that, within this challenging form, George manages to include elements of spirituality, the cosmos, climate change, and an elk!

Special Award:
Special Awards are given when we feel a submitter or a particular piece has somehow resonated something that takes us out of a normal category award. The two *Special Awards* this year go to two people for very different reasons:

The Gift of an Hour with Grandkids, A Collection of Senryū and Haiku by Mike Nierste.

Mike gave us a mini-collection of ten poems, capturing both the joys and everyday reality of a particular time in one's life, time with grandchildren. The ten poems are each beautifully written in *senryū* and *haiku* forms, and while each poem can stand alone, we feel that they deserve special recognition as a collection.

Ndaba Sibanda is an international writer, bringing new political and social perspectives to CEArts and *The Polk Street Review*, submitting new styles and variety of genres. Ndaba's continued support for several years through multiples entries has broadened *The Polk Street Review*'s borders and been instrumental in creating our CEArts global community.

Category Awards:

Artwork Images:

First Place: ***A Gift of Parental Love*** by Kristine Staley

Second Place: ***Winter on the Mountains*** by Jerry Dreesen

Third Place: ***Anima's Dream*** by Kristine Staley

Prose:

First Place: ***The Fateful Hour*** by Patrick Kalahar

Second Place: ***For Holly Middleton*** by Kitty O'Doherty

Third Place: ***Retirement*** by George W. Wolfe

Honorable Mention: ***An Hour Drive with My Brother*** by Leah Leach

Honorable Mention: ***Oak Strength*** by Gail Mehlan

Poetry/Lyric:

First Place: ***untiltled 2*** by B. Monét

Second Place: ***Stay-at-Home Sheep*** by Jenny Kalahar

Third Place: ***untitled 2*** by Z. Rose

Honorable Mention: ***An Extra Hour*** by David Allen

Honorable Mention: ***This Hour*** by Deborah Petersen

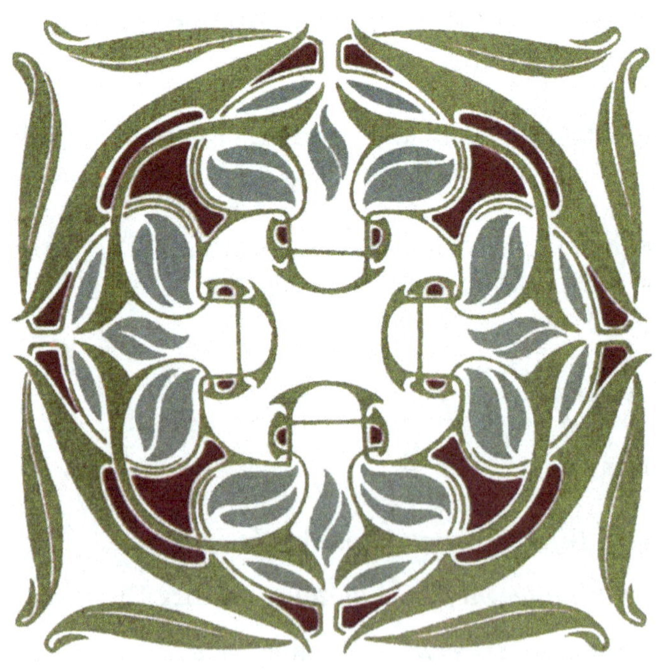

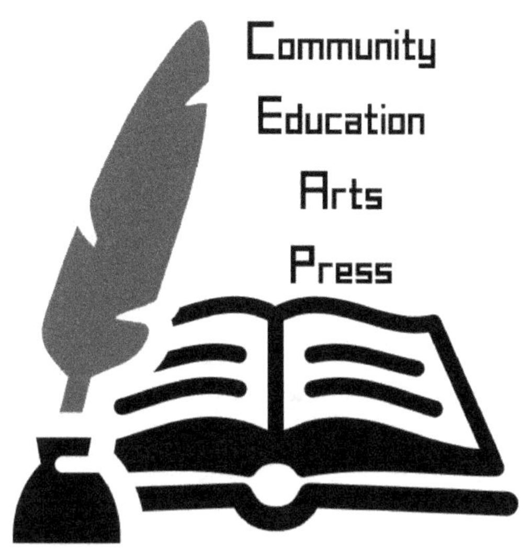

The Polk Street Review is published by
Community • Education • Arts Press
a division of
Community • Education • Arts, Inc.
Noblesville, IN 46060
CEArts.org
info@cearts.org

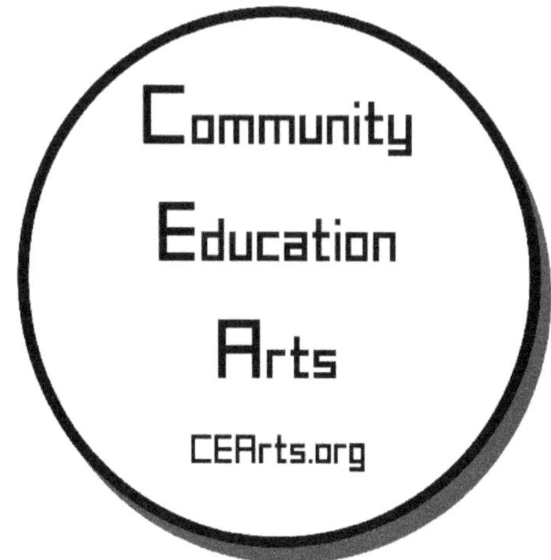

www.ingramcontent.com/pod-product-compliance
Lightning Source LLC
LaVergne TN
LVHW010613110826
845149LV00003B/899

* 9 7 8 0 9 9 9 8 8 5 8 7 1 *